ABOUT TH

John Bishop was born in Heswall on the Wirral, where the nearby Hilbre Island (school trip), Mersey ferries and North Wales triggered his interest in islands, ferry travel and mountains. Supporting Tranmere Rovers from an early age enabled him to empathise with the often-disappointed history of Greece.

A College Principal in Birmingham before retirement, he found the Greek islands a source of tranquillity during holidays and before long one island led to another...

Greek lessons at the Brasshouse Language Centre in Birmingham mean that, after twenty years or so and, despite the excellent teaching, his dream of managing to understand a female Greek TV newsreader as she speaks at twice the speed of sound still remains on the distant horizon.

Having published three novels – the second being 'Love, Freedom or Death', about the WW2 resistance in Crete – he now lives in Codsall, near Wolverhampton, from where he visits Greece as often as possible, returning to the favourites but always looking for new ones to try.

In the meantime, he hopes, in vain, no doubt, that Britain will acknowledge the failings, as well as the successes, of its past, accept its current place in the world and get round to returning the Parthenon marbles.

Email: john.bishop55@btinternet.com
Website: johnbishopauthor.wordpress.com

WILL THERE BE TOILETS ON DELOS?

A PERSONAL GUIDE TO THE GREEK ISLANDS*
FOR THE NERVOUS TRAVELLER

JOHN BISHOP

Ans: Yes, but the Gents is usually locked. Try the Sacred Mountain.

*Well, some of them, sixty or so do for you?

Matador
9 Priory Business Park,
Wistow Road, Kibworth Beauchamp,
Leicestershire. LE8 0RX
Tel: 0116 279 2299
Email: books@troubador.co.uk
Web: www.troubador.co.uk/matador
Twitter: @matadorbooks

ISBN 978 1 8004 6508 4

British Library Cataloguing in Publication Data.
A catalogue record for this book is available from the British Library.

Printed and bound in the UK by TJ Books LTD, Padstow, Cornwall
Typeset in 11pt Minion Pro by Troubador Publishing Ltd, Leicester, UK

Matador is an imprint of Troubador Publishing Ltd

MIX
Paper from
responsible sources
FSC
www.fsc.org
FSC® C013056

For Tom, Jess, Liv and Edwyn

Keep on Roaming

CONTENTS

ARE YOU A NERVOUS TRAVELLER?

You must suspect so or you wouldn't be reading this. Just to be sure:

- Does the thought of visiting a foreign country give you palpitations?
- Do you check the plane involved isn't a 737Max?
- Do you search in detail about where you're going – a year in advance?
- Have you re-checked the tickets to ensure you've not made a mistake?
- Are you really certain your passport has enough months left on it?

Not bad, but

- Do you have a phobia about the alarm's not working?
- Or whether you'll pick up a throat infection on the plane?
- Are you always ready far too soon?

These are all very well but normal enough. If you're a genuinely nervous traveller, you need a bit more.

Like:

- Have you not only ensured you've got enough foreign currency but also that it's secreted into at least three pockets to reduce the risk of theft?
- Does your hand luggage contain spare smalls in case your checked-in luggage goes astray on the flight?
- Do you worry that if you're given a window seat, you might not be able to get to the toilets (On the plane, not Delos. That comes later)?
- Do you keep muttering 'You can't be too careful' in your sleep?

If the answer to **these** questions was Yes, you could be the genuine article.

On the other hand, you may just be an obsessive worrier who'd be a pain in the neck to go on holiday with anywhere. Consider carefully whether Skegness might not be a better option for you. Greece has enough problems.

However, if you're determined, then the Greek Islands could be the place for you.

It won't be kill or cure and let's face it, you actually like the frisson, don't you?

It's called adventure. With a small 'a'. But better not to get too bold.

WHY THE
GREEK ISLANDS?

I t's personal, didn't I say? I've been a nervous traveller since being terrified by the possibility of jellyfish at Prestatyn in 1955. Prior to that I was just nervous. And I wasn't even aware of the threat of nuclear destruction then.

Flying, of course, was another matter. It was 1982 before I overcame the fear of it engendered by the Munich Air Crash of 1958. I still won't fly in February.

I could have travelled overland, I suppose. Eco-tourism before it was invented. There was the 'Magic Bus' that got you from London to Athens in only 48 hours or so. Naturally I was too nervous to try this (are you thinking 'Wimp'?) – the reputation of the Yugoslav roads was enough deterrent. Any excuse…

So it was 1982 when I first set foot on Crete. At 10pm one April night. And standing outside the terminal, under some trees (long since concreted over), it was the scent of orange blossom (or lemon, who cared?) that did it. I was caught.

You should be so lucky.

Nearly twenty years later and before I retired I read somewhere that there are 166 inhabited Greek islands (in fact, if you discount those inhabited by three people and a goat it's more like half that). By then I'd visited ten. A note of clarification here: 'visited' for me means set foot on – no, not running down the gangplank and back up; in any case you'd probably need to buy a new ticket before they'd let you re-board – while for some aficionados it means spend a night on. But life's too short.

I quickly progressed into the thirties. One characteristic of the domestic Greek ferry system is that from Piraeus the lines spread out like the spokes of a wheel. So, it's easy in a fortnight to cover several islands in a chain. What's less easy aka almost impossible is to cut across from one chain to the next. At some point, therefore, the speed at which you notch up islands slows. I also decided that some islands drew me back – Crete fifty times but also Karpathos and Amorgos a clutch of times and a few others more than once – the triumph of quality over quantity. An unexpected bonus, the more you go to the more the nerves improve. OK, scoff, if you must.

So that's the answer to the question why. Still up for it?

Obviously, there'll be other questions that intrude, if you're feeling tempted. For instance, Isn't Greece, like, another country? There's no denying it. However, the traditional British phobias about 'funny' food, the water and the plumbing can be consigned to the (large) dustbin of our prejudices. 'Greek-style' is a familiar supermarket epithet, even if it skirts the Trades Descriptions Act, while moussaka (the stress is on the end if you don't want to give away your ignorance) is ubiquitous. As for the water, it's drinkable almost everywhere and if your stomach is as nervous as the rest of you, bottled mineral water is easy to find, while the plumbing is universally like ours.

Well, almost.

There is one point to mention here. Paper mustn't be flushed down the pan, but put into the bin beside it. Okay, calm down. The bin often has a lid and will be emptied daily anyway. You'll soon get used to it. (And here's a tip to stop you forgetting: when you stand up, put the toilet lid down at once). The reason for this – to us, rather bizarre, custom – is usually given as because of narrow pipes. Paper may block them and, before you know it, it won't only be your nerves feeling watery.

This explanation has always struck me as a touch thin. Given the amount of development in Greece in the last fifty years, wouldn't you think somebody might have considered installing a wider version? The real reason, I suspect, has more to do with only discharging organic material into the … wherever it goes (aka the sea?). Until Greece's carbon footprint is revealed to be scarred by the burning of toilet paper, there's unlikely to be any change. And given their love of cars…

Let's hope you've got this trauma under control before setting off for Skegness. That just leaves the matter of the language. Or rather the alphabet.

If you're panicking about this, consider three things: first, when did Brits ever worry about not being understood by the natives? If in doubt, just shout. Secondly, and more to the point, English is now almost universal: in some parts of Greece, if you speak Greek these days, they'll either be pathetically grateful – Gosh, somebody's taking the trouble to speak our language – or suspicious ie 'What's your game?'

And third, if you haven't already switched off, the Greek language is not actually that different from the English (ie

Roman) one. There are only about five letters that don't appear in the Roman alphabet. Okay, the fact that whoever made the original transfer from Greek to Roman managed to convey β ie v as b doesn't help or that there are four letters that are e; nor that it's an inflected language – with cases (never mind), that became too difficult for us Anglo-Saxons in about 1450. Throw in the fact that there is a more formal version of modern Greek floating about and that the Greeks tend to speak extra fast and… I'm beginning to see your point.

However, before you re-book that ticket to Skegness (where you might need even more foreign languages to get by) there are a couple of tips that should see you through. One is that as there's no letter B in Greek (it's V, remember, above, unless your short-term memory is so bad nervousness is the least of your worries), the sound is made using the two letters μ (M) and π (P, remember pie from School? The Greeks got everywhere. Never mind, again). As the Greek letter R looks like our P (I shouldn't have got you into this) the word for 'bar' will look like μπαρ. This could be a recipe for a temperance holiday but frankly you're not likely to confuse a bar with the Women's Institute anyway, are you?

Just to cheer you up before moving on from this mistaken attempt at reassurance, I once turned up at a hotel in central Crete and said, in Greek, to the young woman who was in charge at the time that I'd booked a room with Stephano. The look of anguish on her face probably mirrors yours as she stuttered 'Do you speak English?' She was from Moldova.

Enough of the negatives. Remember the orange blossom scent. Oh, that was me, wasn't it, but that's the point. Greece and the islands especially have everything you could possibly need, including the entire thirty series of 'Only Fools and

Horses' playing on an endless loop (In a μπαρ) if you choose the right (ie wrong) place. Incidentally, you know more Greek than you think. As much as twenty per cent of English is of Greek origin. Many medical and scientific words are Greek: if you're geriatric, for instance (no offence intended), the word is just the Greek 'old' and 'medical'. And as the Bible was originally written in Greek it's a rich repository of Greek. 'Genesis' simply means 'birth' while Peter was called the rock because his name – Petros – means stone.

So, some positives. There are plenty more.

The colours, especially the blues of sea and sky (hence the colours of the national flag), but also the variety of shades of green – from pines to olives – and those of sand and rock. Years ago a boss asked me what I did when I went to Greece. 'Gaze at the amazing beauty of the landscape,' I replied. She looked at me as if I was mad. Right, of course, but isn't madness better than nervousness? Suit yourself.

The food (go on, put your inhibitions aside: the menus will probably have an English section); the wine – I only drink open wine, in a jug and possibly out of a large plastic bag in the back, although in the less touristed areas it may well be their own and certainly additive-free. Only once have I had bad open wine. A connoisseur? Er…

And the people, always interesting and in many cases surprisingly anglophile – surprisingly because of the way we've treated them over the years. In some places we still owe the goodwill to Lord Byron (Vyron, that is) who did little more than raise funds for the liberation movement then come over and die of fever in 1821. Some years ago I was reading a biography of Byron in a taverna in Rhodes Old Town and when the proprietor asked me what it was I added that he wasn't a

7

very nice man. The look of instant shock I got made me realise my gaffe. 'To the ladies,' I added hastily. To the Greeks it's your intentions that matter; the outcome depends on other things. (And they did gain their independence ten years later)

The name of Churchill doesn't have the same cachet. Quite the opposite in many quarters. His virulent anti-communism meant that having bartered with Stalin for Greece to remain outside the Iron Curtain, he engineered a Civil War, leading to right-wing control for decades and the exclusion of anyone with vaguely left-wing connexions from all civil employment until 1982. The fact that our reputation survives is often because somebody worse followed us. During the evacuation of Crete after our failure to defend the island in the Battle of 1941 we were roundly abused for our refusal to arm the islanders and our desertion. It was only when the Nazi reprisals started that our failings began to be forgotten.

Similarly, we began the Civil War in 1946 funding the right-wing forces, many of whom had been Nazi sympathisers, only to find that our post-war destitution meant we could no longer afford it. The Americans, under the Truman doctrine of fighting communism everywhere, took over and their use of napalm in the Grammos mountains finally drove the remnants of the communist guerrillas over the border into Yugoslavia. Yet memories linger. Twenty years ago, in conversation with a young Greek man on Amorgos, he mentioned Americans then stopped himself and added (in English) 'Oh, I should say, the fucking Americans.' In the 80s feelings ran so high that their bases metamorphosed into NATO ones overnight.

What I particularly like is the simplicity (Yes, alright, you'd already guessed that I must be pretty simple). There's no fake prettiness, well, not much anyway. The Greek islands are the peaks of mountain ranges thrust up from the sea, rocky and often bare. Nature unadorned and uncompromising. And a life that was generally hard reflects that.

Don't forget the history. Four thousand years of it. Never mind the roots of literature, democracy and philosophy. More than enough to make you forget your nerves as you, too, gaze in wonder.

One clarification here: this book covers about sixty *inhabited* Greek islands and there are a number I haven't visited, either because they didn't attract me or because getting there has been beyond me. There are also any number that are uninhabited, a few, like Makronissi and Giaros, because as former prison islands they have been put off limits; most are too arid to support much habitation (though as in the case of Halki, among a few others, a bit of aridity shouldn't get in the way of making money. These days water tankers can make up for the absence of a decent water source.)

And another: island names. I've noted in the Ionian islands the predominance still of two names. In fact, it's a widespread phenomenon and some islands have been through a number, from antiquity via various conquests in which the occupier brought its own name, often with the Greek original re-emerging later. And in Greek the current name may differ from the westernised one. All adding to the fascination. No, not just to increase your sense of disorientation…

PLANNING

However, as a nervous traveller, you won't be satisfied with a bit of reassurance before you go. You'll need research. In the past this might have meant going through a few dozen brochures to compare the place you were considering before making a choice. And perhaps lashing out on a guide-book whose advice you'd imbibe with a recklessness and trust absent from the rest of your life. Nowadays the problem has become slightly different and, dare I say it, more stressful. Information overload. Where once you could set off full of confidence (ha, ha, ha) but really in unblissful ignorance, today, thanks to the internet, there could be pitfalls lurking everywhere in your mind. Sorting the unacknowledged marketing guff from the review comments posted while under the effects of relationship breakdown (no, not yours. Yet) while ploughing through the 23,000 online criticisms will make your head spin faster than an excess of raki.

The answer? As ever, take a deep breath. Sample a few, with scepticism. Get a general feeling. Remember that a guide-book is a guide, it might be as personal as this. (And so, a licence to ignore? Thanks a lot)

If you're that nervous about launching into the unknown, a package holiday may make sense. Although the number of Greek specialists has shrunk in recent years there are some – Sunvil and Olympic Holidays in particular – which have good track records.

As for guide-books, people will have their favourites. I've always found Rough Guides fairly sound. Much of their offer is now online but the Rough Guide to Crete is usually re-issued every couple of years and there's a recent one for the Greek Islands. Both are a bit slimmer and more upmarket than previously – again thanks to the internet's shrinking the market, but a book does have advantages over the internet: you can glance at different pages in hand at once.

One reason guide-books have slimmed down is that internet booking sites provide a wide range of accommodation options, together with prices. This, of course, reduces the nervous fear of there being nothing available (if you're travelling under your own steam) as you can pre-book. And with Booking.com a free cancellation option means that if a virus hits, you have the chance to change plans. These websites don't usually cover the cheaper room options but guide-books rarely did either. You just had to trust to luck – and not worry about your nerves. Ha, ha, ha.

There was a very useful guide to the Greek Islands, until 2013: 'Greek Island Hopping', edited by Frewin Poffley and published annually by Thomas Cook. Although the publishers did little more than change the date each year (though see below) and its ferry timetables were really only illustrative, its summaries of each island and the port maps were invaluable. You might still find a secondhand 2013 copy available on the internet.

There is a case for having an up-to-date guidebook, especially for timetables, although smartphones now ensure that you ought not to be working to out-of-date information. Several years ago, on Sikinos, the map in my previous year's copy of 'Greek Island Hopping' indicated a ticket office at the port. When I went to buy a ticket couple of hours (note how nerves can be useful!) before the ferry was due, I discovered that the office had moved up to the Hora, on the hill, several kilometres away. Fortunately, the previous day I'd found the old kalderimi (footpath) from the port to the Hora and after busting a gut uphill and frantically scouring the narrow alleys of the Hora, I got a ticket for the ferry just in time. Had I not been tight-fisted (worse than being nervous?) and bought it, the current edition did show the correct location.

For ferry timetables the gtp.gr website provides reliable detail, though for forward planning it can be irritating. While you can now book a flight to Greece up to a year ahead, in many cases there's no ferry information available until late April. So booking a flight risks the ferry you want not running until a day later. The delay is probably because until then the ferry companies are still playing hardball with the government over subsidies.

COVID actually also helped the spread of smartphones since you needed a QR code on one in 2020 to enter Greece in the short interval between lockdowns. They should in addition enable you to keep track of where you are and what you want to do, though in the absence of a signal in some remote spot they might add to the pressure on your nerves.

Post-Brexit there's some uncertainty about roaming charges in Greece. Shortly before Brexit and on the west coast of the Greek island of Ikaria, my phone greeted me with 'Welcome to Turkey' ie outside the EU, where limits on roaming charges don't apply. Given that on the east coast of Ikaria, and therefore nearer to Turkey, I was apparently still under Greek coverage, this was puzzling. But then the Turks under Erdogan have been playing fast and loose in the Mediterranean for some time. They're after the oil and gas reserves. And a few bob from BT is probably needed since Erdogan has trashed the economy.

A quick note on Turkey: what is now Greece was part of the Ottoman Empire for several centuries. While lauded for its religious tolerance (as long as you coughed up the taxes), its laissez-faire attitude extended to allowing local despots to behave as they wished and this behaviour was often arbitrary and vicious. In Crete, especially, this led to periodic uprisings, either before or after massacres, and ultimately to the demand for independence. And remember what I said above about memories.

This historic enmity was fuelled further after WW1 when Lloyd George was instrumental in giving Greece the role of policing western Anatolia, still largely Greek-speaking. Unfortunately, a right-wing Greek government saw this as an opportunity to regain lost territories, were lured into the interior by Kemal Pasha, who then turned on the Greek army and drove them back into the sea, in the process wiping out Smyrna, one of the great cities of the near east. (Following this disaster, a number of leaders, including the father of the Duke of Edinburgh, were sentenced to death, though he was later reprieved)

So, while the azure waters off Turkey may appeal, there is much blood in it.

HOW TO
GET THERE

If you've chosen the package route, this is straightforward: you select an airport convenient for you that serves your destination. If you're travelling independently ie flight only, this will depend on where you're going: many Greek islands have no direct flights from the UK, certainly not from provincial airports, so you'll probably have to fly to Athens or one of the island hubs and travel onward from there. Here the options, or complications, are varied.

Hang on, you may be saying, what about the environment? Shouldn't we be avoiding air travel? 'Ha, ha, isn't that objection really about your nerves?' I'm tempted to retort. You can indeed travel overland to Greece, even though no enterprising coach company has replaced the aforementioned Magic Bus. The more traditional route is by train to Bari in Italy then ferry to Patras in the northern Peloponnese and onward by coach to Athens. An alternative goes from Milan via Budapest and possibly Sofia before reaching Thessaloniki in northern Greece. There is talk of a new Orient Express to Budapest in a couple of years' time but, as you'd only be worried about being murdered on it, it's perhaps best discounted.

These options take one or two days and you've still got onward travel to the islands so you'll have to weigh carefully your climate-saving inclinations. There's also the small matter of frequent changes of train or ferry that won't soothe your nerves.

Back to the main point: selling your soul for a four-hour flight. The number of islands with direct flights from UK regional airports is limited: Crete, Rhodes, Corfu, Kefalonia, Kos, Skiathos, for instance. A couple more have direct flights only from London. And there are direct flights to Athens, the main hub for flights or ferries to the islands, from London, Manchester or a few UK places as remote as Anafi.

If you don't live near these and your nerves won't stand motorway travel – smart motorways, anyone? – then flying with one of the main European flag-carriers – KLM, Lufthansa, Air France – is your best option, though involving at least one transfer on the continent. Various websites will list the choices. Again the journey will take longer, though Birmingham-Munich-Athens only involved a 45 minute stopover. Yes, you'd be worrying if there was time to make the connexion and, the first time I did it, Munich Airport's boast that they could do a transfer in 35 minutes seemed optimistic, especially as the coach from the plane to the terminal appeared to be setting off onto the German autobahn network. Never fear, they did it. (And their toilets had toilet seat covers, another worry for you to ditch).

There is, however, one fly in this ointment: Brexit. Increased border checks to get into the EU mean that a quick transfer may be a thing of the past. Agghhh.

You've reached Athens, now what? Until a few years ago the 10pm BA/Olympic flight from Heathrow (via National

Express coach) arrived in Athens at about 4am, giving you plenty of time (after luggage collection) to catch the 6am bus down to Piraeus for a 7.30 ferry (the journey taking an hour). However, the flights are now earlier and the prospect of a four-hour wait in the airport (smart though it is, a legacy of an Olympics investment that has paid off) is hardly enticing. The day flights will generally involve you in an overnight stay somewhere: if you want convenience the choice on the airport is the Sofitel – an arm-and-a-leg job as it has a monopoly, though very plush and comfortable – or a bench in Departures (the ones in Arrivals don't allow for lying down).

Hotels in central Athens are still fairly pricey and you'll have Metro trips (from the airport, very efficient though your nerves might suffer if you've read about the ubiquity of pickpockets) before your onward trip.

If your onward trip is a flight, the main hassle is the Aegean Airlines check-in system which will remind you that the word 'chaos' is Greek – the ch being the Greek letter X (Khee, of which more later). This is mainly because about seventeen internal flights, to every Greek island with an airport, seem to leave at 11.30am and there's one queue. Online check-in can reduce this a bit as you only have to drop off a bag (travelling light might be a nerves-free alternative).

If you're going on by ferry then you need to get to Piraeus, the main port of Greece, Rafina or more rarely Lavrio. The last two, though smaller and both reachable by bus from the airport, only serve relatively few islands.

Buses to Piraeus are generally at least hourly and quick; at peak times it may be standing room only with the risk, at severely busy times, of inadvertent impregnation from close proximity of the kind usually found on the Tube or Tokyo underground. (No, don't worry, it won't happen to you. Probably. Just learn to say sorry in thirteen European, hang on, make that world, languages) In your panic, remember to cancel your ticket: you're more likely to get fined for not doing this than for any charges of indecent assault.

The bus used to go into the port but I'm not sure it does now (Nervous threat alert). Follow the crowd, which probably means getting off across the road (It's a six-lane highway but before you press the Panic alert, press the crossing button: there's a controlled crossing). Assuming you know which island you're aiming for, you've probably done your research into which Gate it's leaving from (Piraeus is a big port but… no, no, don't press the P… again) and most have ticket booths nearby. Just make sure you book for the ferry you want, not one they want to sell you. The ferries generally show their destinations and departure time above the stern. Once on board you can leave your luggage in the racks, usually marked for particular destinations, though reclaiming it if the rack is full can be a struggle. (Oh, no, I've done it again) If it's a rucksack, you can keep it with you, as you can a case but since you may have to climb several decks it may not be worth the effort.

The ferries to Crete and more outlying islands tend to depart from further round the Great Harbour. There's rumoured to be a shuttle bus, but I've never seen a dodo either, except in the Test & Trace context.

So, you're all settled, only worrying where the toilets are (They'll be clearly signed and marked).

All that's left now is – where to go?

WHERE TO GO

Most guide-books divide up their contents geographically for convenience since most of the islands belong to specific groups. However, given that this is personal (Did you snigger 'idiosyncratic' or was it 'barmy'?), I'll start with a couple of the favourites and then proceed, mainly on a geographical basis, from there. As there are a few favourites on the mainland, I'll throw them in too. We'll start with

CRETE

The Great Island. Largest of the Greek islands. 185 miles long and anything from ten to forty wide, cut by three massive mountain ranges, with summits of 8000 feet, and plenty of lesser but still imposing peaks besides. Stunning scenery and enough history, both ancient and modern, to make you forget your nerves for the whole of your stay. It is indeed almost another country in itself.

A word of warning (no, not about your bloody nerves): don't try to 'do' it all in one visit. By all means sample a few different parts but, say, renting a hire car so you can persuade yourself you've seen it all is self-defeating. You'll end up frazzled, or, worse... You need to come back. Several times.

Because of its size and the fact that there are two main airports, it makes sense to deal with Crete in sections, east, central and west, although the north and south coasts also come into the matter. The 'News of the World' (not RIP) used to claim of itself that all human life was there. The same could be said of Crete. You can probably find something to suit everybody's taste or lack of it somewhere in Crete. We'll be avoiding the latter. And start in

WESTERN CRETE

The main city of Western Crete, Chania, is arguably the island's most attractive one, with its old town set on the former Venetian harbour. A word on its pronunciation, which is 'Han-yah', the stress on the end and the Ch being our old friend the Greek letter X (Khee). On a bus to Hania (as I'm now going to transcribe it) a Swedish woman in front of me had hysterics when the conductor announced that it was the bus for Han-yah. 'But I'm going to Charnia!' she shrieked. It took some time to convince her it was the same place. (Oh, God, that wasn't you, was it?)

Both port and airport of Hania are some miles to the east, the port on Souda Bay, one of the great natural harbours of the Mediterranean, for ferries from Piraeus, and the airport at Akrotiri, which overlooks the bay. Until about twenty years ago the airport was principally a military one, with a few charter flights tolerated. Having grown gradually, it was given a major overhaul a couple of years ago (big EU grant – perhaps we ought to join) and is now very impressive. Still considerably smaller than the island's main airport at the capital, Heraklion, it provides a more hassle-free experience. Besides the military presence its other major drawback in the past – the lack of a bus service from Hania – has also now been addressed, with hourly buses at a tenth of the taxi fare. The journey by either takes about the same time: half an hour or so. However, you probably get a more dramatic introduction to Crete from the front of a taxi as it turns left at the end of the airport road and the sheer wall of the mountain Zourva looms ahead. The shape of things to come and worth the twenty-five euros fare.

HANIA

If you're intending to move on by bus, especially an early one, from Hania, your nerves will no doubt require you to stay close to the bus station, so that the risk of missing it will be reduced. As there are two hotels next door and one across the road to the rear this is hardly a difficulty. I settle for the Arkadi, on Square 1866, about three minutes away (note the boldness). From a high floor room (4ᵗʰ?) on the front, the 180 degree views sweep from the harbour on your left all the way round to the White Mountains, often still snow-covered in early summer.

The harbour is a mere ten minutes' walk from here and on your walk down you'll pass the bright new modern art gallery, the so-called 'Leather Street' and the small archaeological museum in an atmospheric former church building. Whiling away the time is not difficult, with a coffee along the quay, passing the excellent Mediterraneo bookshop, well-stocked with English language books about Crete, on the way to the

Fortress which houses the Naval Museum and, on the top floor, a museum of the Battle of Crete, now rather in need of an update. Or you can stroll round the inner harbour, coming eventually to the lighthouse you'll have seen opposite you as you reached the quay. In this direction, past the former mosque (usually with art displays) and trendy cocktail bars, you'll also pass, behind the new Theodorakis concert hall, in which he's now unlikely to play, the Faka Taverna, with excellent Fava (Yes, time to experiment – think humus but served warm) and Boureki (ditto – cheese and sliced potato pie) and good red open wine.

The north-western coast beyond Hania was slower to develop than that to the east of Heraklion but is now catching up fast, the section from Kato (Lower) Stalos to Maleme increasingly splattered by large hotels. However, up the hill from Kato Stalos are some studios which keep you above the agglomerations below, with views out to sea a bonus. From here you can walk through the olive groves in the hills behind and down among the orange groves beyond. Although villas are colonising the area, progress is fairly slow as yet. An hour's walk will bring you to Galatas, scene of a major defensive stand by the Allies and a rousing, though ultimately futile, New Zealand bayonet charge during the Battle, commemorated by a memorial in the village square. It's mainly road walking but the chances of seeing a vehicle are small. If that's too much, the road train that runs along the old coast road and then into the hills is surprisingly good, stopping at Lake Agia and visiting an orange grove.

Buses will give you access to many places from Hania, the blue and white local buses leaving from 1866 Square (with ticket kiosk) and serving the areas closer to the town; the green buses leaving the bus station (recently refurbished), which has printed timetables readily available, and covering the whole of western Crete besides linking with the rest of the island to the east. A bendy-bus runs along the north coast as far as Kolimbari (Pay on board).

If it's your first visit to Crete, it's worth taking a couple of coach trips to get a feel for the island without the hassle of trying to find your own way. The latter is potentially more rewarding but, thinking of your nerves, best left till another time.

There are two longer trips you can make yourself from Hania using the buses and later boats. The first is the 8.30 bus to Kissamos (taking about an hour and a half) for the boat trip to Balos. This is touted as a trip to the beautiful beach at Balos and always sounded a bit tacky but it's actually worth doing. Kissamos is technically Kastelli Kissamos but generally known by the latter name. At the bus station ask for the port and a return ticket: the bus goes into the port and will be waiting there on your return at about 6pm (Nerves can be parked). The boat trip calls at the island of Gramvousa, where's there's a castle you can walk up to and the boat has no shortage of food and drink (There's none at Balos). Aside from the interest of the journey itself, which is probably more of a highlight than the beach, getting to Balos by car involves a lengthy walk down from the car parks above it (and back up!).

The BIG trip of course is the Samaria Gorge. If you're nervous about being stranded somewhere on the south coast, you can do this with a guide on an organised tour. It will cost you more and although you can't really get lost in the Gorge, it may give you reassurance about the bus leg back to Hania. Essentially the trip involves a bus or coach journey of about an hour up to the Omalos plateau, at 4000 feet, from where you descend into the Gorge and walk for thirteen kilometres to the sea at Agia Roumeli – anything from four to seven hours. From there a boat takes you in another hour to Hora Sfakion (generally known as Sfakia, stress on the last 'a') and from Sfakia the bus or coach takes you the two hours or so back to Hania (or wherever you started from since coach trips start from many parts of the island.) Tough trainers or preferably boots are needed – Cretan paths are rocky.

If you're not up to the trek involved, organised trips are offered called 'Samaria the Lazy Way'. Probably a bit insulting though it means not having to get up quite as early as for the full trip. A coach takes you down to Sfakia in time for the 10.30 ferry to Agia Roumeli, where you have about five hours in which to walk part of the way into the Gorge (or sit eating and drinking, or sunbathing all afternoon). You might get as far as the famous Iron Gates where the Gorge narrows to a few metres with the cliffs rising a thousand feet above, but you're unlikely to have time to penetrate further into the really deep recesses. Sigh of relief? Who's a wimp now?

While you can 'do' the Gorge as a day trip, it and the areas above, below and around it really need more time if you're to get their full glory. I'll deal with the descent of the Gorge in detail later as part of this but however you do it – DON'T HURRY! This may seem counterintuitive if (as you're bound to be) you're anxious about missing the boat at the end. The trek can be completed in four hours if you hurry but, assuming you start off at about 9am, you have eight hours before the boat leaves at 5.30. You may feel obliged to keep up with a group if you're in one, but remember the Virginia Woolf quote from 'Mrs Dalloway': 'Nothing could be slow enough, nothing take too long.' The Gorge deserves time. The bigger problem is keeping in between the crowds: there can be a thousand or more people in there on any one day and, while that will provide you with security, it might be bad for the nerves in other ways.

South from Hania

The road to the Omalos Plateau ascends first to Lakkoi, perched on a ridge with vertiginous drops either side. There are rooms, though bear in mind that from your balcony you'll be staring down several hundred feet. If you stop for coffee, note the memorials to the resistance in WW2 and earlier, but don't neglect the churchyard nearby, with a memorial to those villagers deported to Mauthausen by the Nazis.

From Lakkoi there is reputed to be a path down to Meskla in the valley behind, from where a road walk will take you up via Zourva to Theriso, famed for its role in the Cretan independence movement at the beginning of the twentieth century, and thence down the Theriso Gorge (by road) where you might be hoping to pick up a bus. Your nervousness about this might be confirmed here ie it won't come.

Down in the valley that gouges its way southwards from Lakkoi was once a path used for moving sheep up to the plateau for the summer but any trace of it is difficult to follow and far too bad for the nerves: the failure to maintain many traditional paths is one of Crete's lost opportunities but then having to walk was a sign you were poor.

The best guide to walking in these mountains is 'Crete: The White Mountains' by Loraine Wilson (Cicerone). Good even for the faint-hearted – to read, at least.

So the way south is via the road, winding, ascending and also with vertiginous drops to the side. Your nerves will feel the benefit of not driving this way. In a vehicle you'd perhaps also miss the memorial halfway up to Andreas Vandoulas and the New Zealand guerrilla leader Dudley Perkins, ambushed nearby in February 1944. Since they straightened the road the memorial has been reset and is less obvious now.

After the final climb you'll see the plateau open out below you to the mountains further on. The village, mainly a collection of small hotels, lies just before the perimeter road splits, one way, left, leading up to the head of the Gorge, the other, right, taking you to the turn down to the Hania-Souyia road or the Agia Irini Gorge.

OMALOS

A stay at the village is well worthwhile, the Hotel Neos Omalos, run by Giorgos Drakoulakis and family, is a favourite, its pleasant rooms complemented by the excellent food. The early morning air, deliciously cold, is another bonus. Giorgos will also transfer you to the head of the Gorge, unless your masochism (another alternative to the N word) demands that you walk the three kilometres or so there.

You may have to walk that route a few times anyway since, while you can ask the bus driver to drop you in the village, the struggle to extricate your bag from the generally over-stocked boot may not make it worth the effort. In any case, turning up at 9am will probably mean the room isn't ready, so you'd have to go out and walk. Staying on the bus to the head of the Gorge, known as Xyloskala, enables you to have a drink at the café there (surprisingly reasonably-priced given its monopoly position and clientele, most of whom will never return) or even visit the Museum of the Gorge, though the last time I found it open was 2004.

An advantage of walking to and from Omalos village is that the vast bulk of Gingilos will dominate your sight and suffuse you with wonder. (A good cure for nerves)

From the café area there are a couple of substantial hikes, other than the Gorge itself. The first might not be easy on your nerves. This is the route up Gingilos, the mountain whose massive granite wall towers above the west side of the Gorge.

The path starts from behind the café, passing the taverna above and ascending steeply in zigzags before levelling out for a bit. Already there are extensive views back across the plateau and into the Gorge. The first nerve-wracking section (OK, only for wimps like me) comes when you need to pass beneath a rock arch, in itself probably solid enough but it's approached down a slope, the narrow path falling quite sharply and with a further drop, of a few hundred feet, down into the Gorge itself. You can turn back here without any shame. (Well, I felt none)

Last time I braved this I turned back a bit further on where a landslide had broken up the path. It was probably negotiable without much risk as the boulders were large, but I didn't fancy it. Winter storms can play havoc with paths everywhere in the mountains and, given the absence of money for regular maintenance, it's left to local volunteers to do what they can.

After following the side of the Gorge, the path then climbs in easy zigzags up to the saddle leading to the summit of Gingilos. From here you can peer down into the Tripiti

Gorge and the true wild lands. Apparently, there's a path that traverses it and eventually comes to Koustoyerako, the village above Souyia and legendary home to some of the most celebrated resistance fighters against the Germans in WW2. The sight of the gorge was enough for me.

From the saddle it's mainly a scramble up to the summit, watching out for any of the bottomless pits on the way (no, you won't either). You'll be at almost seven thousand feet. Even at the café you're higher than the summit of Snowden.

The other walk is less precipitous and takes you up to the Kallergi Refuge via a fairly good path leading to the shepherds' road to the top, a steady pull with no vertiginous edges to the side. At the top you can walk on across the Poria, from where there's an exit from the Gorge, though closed now except for a crazy race that goes down into the Gorge and up this way. Although visitors are strictly forbidden to wander off the main path, there are several ways out of the Gorge – or were, known only to the people who lived there. During the Civil War (1946-9) the remnants of the Communist forces in Crete were driven into the Gorge and, it was believed, therefore trapped, since the main exits were blocked. However, someone knew of a hidden exit and led the survivors eventually to safety via a somewhat perilous route.

After two and a half hours or so this way will bring you to the ridge walk of Melindaou, said to be one of the finest in Europe (no, I haven't – only because from Omalos the distance for the round trip would have been too far, you realise?) If you turn right at the top, you'll see the refuge with a viewing platform beside it. Return to Omalos is via the shepherds' road/dirt track down to the main road.

Before dealing in more detail with the Samaria Gorge, it's worth pointing out that there is an alternative route from the Omalos Plateau down to the south coast. This involves the Agia Irini Gorge, much smaller and shorter than Samaria, as the middle section.

From Omalos village take the right fork when you reach the perimeter road and after forty minutes or so, when it bends to the left towards Xyloskala, take the right fork uphill to the small church of Agios Theodoros. A few hundred metres further on is a decrepit picnic site, in the left-hand corner of which is the start of the path leading down, after a couple of hours, to the head of the Agia Irini Gorge, with a pleasant kafenion before you start. There's not much accessible water in the Gorge and a small ladder to negotiate before you emerge at a taverna, prior to a couple of hours more on the road into Souyia. The first time I did this, in 2002, I went for a drink at a bar and thought I was hallucinating from the effort. The World Cup was on the TV and the score read Belgium 0 England 3.

Souyia is a pleasant, low-key beach resort with some good rooms places and tavernas. To the west a two-hour stroll brings you to the archaeological site of Lissos and from there it's possible to walk on to Paleochora, a further couple of hours away.

Inland and across the dried-up river-bed a dirt track eventually comes out on the road up to Kostouyerako, village of the WW2 resistance and scene of what Patrick Leigh Fermor called 'one of the most spectacular moments of the war' when Costis Paterakis, from high on the cliff above the village square, shot the German machine gunner as he prepared to execute the local women and children.

A long trek eastwards will bring you to Agia Roumeli but it probably needs an overnight stay in the open and the way is far from clear. Not for the nervous. Somewhere on You Tube there's an entertaining description by Stelios Jackson from the Hellenic Bookstore in Kentish Town of an attempt he made from the Agia Roumeli end. It won't soothe your nerves or entice you to try as he got lost and had to call friends from Souyia to come in a boat and rescue him.

THE GORGE OF SAMARIA

Given the coachloads who descend the Gorge it would be easy to sneer at it. However, its difficulty shouldn't be underestimated. The going is generally rough.

In the first hour you descend more than a thousand feet on the so-called Xiloskala (wooden steps), though nowadays the wood is on the (often rickety) handrails. As a nervous traveller you'll have no difficulty taking care.

In total you'll walk about fifteen kilometres because, while the back of the ticket (hold on to it, you need to show it at the exit) shows the distance as 12.8 you've another couple to go outside the Gorge before the sea, although there is a shuttle bus for that part if you've had enough. It took me some years to puzzle out how the Gorge was claimed to be sixteen kilometres long when the ticket and way markers gave the shorter distance. (Yes, substituting 'Dim' besides 'Wimp' for 'Nervous' in the title was considered). The reason, as you'll have guessed immediately, is that, while the full Gorge starts from below the saddle of Gingilos, the dedicated walk only begins at the Xiloskala, three kilometres further down.

Other points to worry you, sorry, I mean enable you to take care: it can be hot down there, especially from July onwards and there's no shade in many places. Early in the season (It only opens on May 1st, unless there's been too much rain – thirty years ago three tourists were drowned after being washed away in a flash flood), the repeated crossing of the river will require you to negotiate sometimes slippery stepping-stones. By early June the water level has usually dropped.

More worryingly there's a section on the descent where you walk through a wire mesh corridor, there being the risk of falling stones: a few years ago a boy was seriously injured by a rock perhaps dislodged by a goat a thousand feet above. If you've been consoled by this protection, a notice at the bottom telling you 'Danger of death: walk quickly' might disabuse you (the Greek means something more like 'get as far away from here as possible'). Being dim, I've never quite worked out how walking quickly would help. In any event, as I said earlier, take it slowly, there is much to admire. (You might think there was a market for helmet hire but the logistics of getting them back up from the bottom is probably too great)

You descend through pines and, if you're lucky, their warm breath will sweeten your way, while opposite you the great wall of Gingilos will tower above and you'll catch views back up to the head of the Gorge and the saddle. As you pass down the Gorge there are changing vistas ahead and above. While the height of the walls at the Iron Gates is lauded, compared to the three thousand-foot heights around you in the upper part of the Gorge, they can seem puny. You'll have guessed that it took me a few visits before I realised that was even where the 'gates' were.

The good news is that there's plenty of drinking water in the Gorge, with springs every two or three kilometres so you don't have to carry much – a litre, I'd say since I reckon to half a litre an hour but a couple of years ago, when it was in the thirties, one of the later water points was dribbling and full of wasps. You do need snacks.

The other good news is that not only are there rest areas, they have toilets! Some guide-books have been a bit sarky about them but compared to most UK outdoor provision they're fine. The main one, in the old village of Samaria, is about halfway down. On one of the buildings a plaque (in Greek) records that in 1941 this was the escape route from the invading Germans of the King of Greece, to be picked up in Agia Roumeli by a British destroyer and on to Egypt. Helped *his* nerves, no doubt.

Once in Agia Roumeli a large beer awaits you, if bathing your feet in the sea doesn't take precedence. You can stay overnight in Agia Roumeli, very peaceful once the hordes have gone and there are coastal walks from there (more later). Above the village is a ruined Turkish fort, if you've not had enough ascent. The Turks never managed to penetrate beyond the Iron Gates into the Gorge, which remained a refuge during their centuries-long occupation.

Boats leave (confusingly, at the same time recently) for Sfakia to the east and Souyia to the west – the larger boat doing the Sfakia run, if you're confused – from where buses take people back to their resorts. If you're lingering down here, the place to stay if you're heading east is Loutro, the only intermediate stop on the way.

If you sit on the left of the boat (port, starboard, who can remember?) from Agia Roumeli to Loutro you'll see the huge

31

peaks louring above, bare rock, nature stripped to its essence. You'll also be following, though unable to pick it out from the boat, the coastal path to Loutro, one of the best coastal walks in Crete.

LOUTRO

Loutro, a few kilometres west of Sfakia and nestling around a small bay below two-thousand-foot cliffs, can only be reached by boat or on foot. This forms a great part of its charm. The Blue House, run by Giorgos, Vangelis and family, provides pleasant rooms with sea views and excellent food served next to the sea – no menu, you go up and look at the displays. The choice is also mind-blowing.

There are basically only two things to do in Loutro: walking or nothing. The former has a variety of options, short or long, flat or ascending. A short, fairly level walk goes west round the headland to Finix or Lykos next door, both of which have tavernas. In fact, that's virtually all they have. In the opposite direction, after a couple of kilometres on a reasonable path above the sea, is Sweetwater Bay, with a sandy beach and a kafenion. (Taxi boats serve Sweetwater and Marmara, beyond Lykos, so these could be covered by the 'nothing' ie sunbathing, swimming, option). A short ascent up the path behind Loutro village would allow you to look around the ruins of the castle.

Slightly longer walks to the west of Loutro, which involve some ascent and descent, would take you to Marmara or Livaniana, the village huddled against the hill to the west, which is where the tarmac road down from the top ends. For both, the easier path starts to the left of the mini market behind the phone kiosk and takes you out across the plateau. For Marmara you can cut down to Lykos (or just visit Lykos or Finix, of course) and go along the beach, but this isn't a good choice for the nervous: you have to climb a small cliff – it's OK going towards Marmara but, returning, the way down isn't clear (it's near the left edge) – and then creep round a rock above the sea. A less stressful alternative involves following the dirt road up towards Livaniana until the bend onto the headland, where there's a blue-marked path (somewhere!) that comes out at the top of an uneven and rocky but safe enough stairway down to the main path. Marmara has a taverna and you can wander up into the lower reaches of the Aradena Gorge (of which more later) if you wish.

For Livaniana, you can follow the dirt road on its circuitous route upwards but the more interesting way is via the old kalderimi – look for red dots on the right not far along the dirt road. Kalderimia were the old main highways between villages and in many cases were almost works of art, with stone-built edges and usually well-paved. Until several years ago, before the tarmac road reached Livaniana, the postman came by ferry to Loutro twice a week and then took the kalderimi up to Livaniana. There has been a kafenion/taverna in Livaniana but whether it survives I'm not sure.

Livaniana has no roads, its houses being linked merely by passageways that ascend the hill. From the top, above the church, you can gaze beyond the Aradena Gorge, not visible from where you are, towards the hamlet of Agias Ioannis on its far side.

From here, for the more adventurous, there are a couple of options, one of moderate length the other a fair pull. As you might expect, neither is entirely nerve-tingling-free.

The first, and slightly easier because it's downhill, starts by going straight ahead from the top, along a dirt track that has a path leading off to the left (it may not be very clear) that zigzags fairly steadily down to the bottom of the Aradena Gorge. Turning left there you will come out at Marmara – but only after descending two huge rockfalls. The first is the more nerve-wracking as the way down over boulders is not that clear. Keep right, I think, but you may come to a precipice. My advice, which I generally fail to follow, is that if it seems as if you've taken the wrong turn, you probably have – turn back and look. The way down is easier to find than the way up: at various times I've ended up in a cave full of goats (who weren't pleased) and struggled to find the way. In fact, after the last time, ascending, a couple of years ago, I put a note in my record book DO NOT REPEAT. However, once past this, the last rockfall is much clearer, the path descending gradually beside the left-hand wall. The Gorge then flattens out and you can admire the towering cliffs either side before you arrive at Marmara and the way back as previously described.

The second has no rockfalls but involves a poor path high against the hillside and a long loop back down to Loutro. Essentially you are cutting off a considerable number of the bends in the tarmac road to reach the plateau. From the top of Livaniana, turn right up a clear, straight path. In a short while this breasts the hill and you look down across a plateau with a small chapel in the distance (from here a further alternative to the previous walk would take you to the chapel and, with your back to its front, aim towards the Gorge. Somewhere there, is an easy descent into the Gorge some way before the arrival point on the previous walk).

For this one, turn right here up a kalderimi in reasonable state which cuts up through the cliff. Ahead of you the path ascends across the face of the mountainside to a stretch of the tarmac road. The path is clear but narrow and in places has fallen away requiring care to get across (You'll have guessed this is the nervy bit). When it reaches the road the path does continue, cutting off the next bend but the going, while safe, is so rocky that a French couple made it ahead of me by following the road. In theory the path then goes across the open scrubland at the top but it's so difficult to find and probably equally difficult underfoot that keeping to the road is preferable, if longer.

Eventually the road meets the Anopolis-Aradena one. By turning right (and leaving exploration of Aradena village for another day – you've still got another three hours to go) you'll come to Anopolis where, again turning right, you'll wind up to the edge of the mountain above Loutro. Descent is about two hours but take care (as if I needed to say it). The path, possibly over a thousand years old, is rocky and uneven – and you'll be tired. There's only one place where it's tricky – thanks to the shepherds' dirt road's cutting through it. The views down to Loutro are magnificent and on a clear day you'll see Gavdos fifty kilometres out to sea, next stop Africa. But remember Wainwright's dictum: 'If you want to look, stop,' to avoid falling over.

The descent you've just made can form the return section of two or three other walks, the simplest being a climb up to Anopolis for lunch (excellent taverna in the Square). An alternative is to climb up to the Anopolis plateau from Sfakia by the old kalderimi, now mainly a dry stream bed, involving the odd climb, and then across the plateau (Anopolis, like

35

many in Greece, is a dispersed village of several smaller settlements) to the Square. In either case, you can't fail to notice the mass of the high mountains behind including, out-of-sight beyond, Pachnes, second-highest peak in Crete by a couple of metres.

It will also be a return leg if you want to visit Aradena village and not make a circular walk by descending the length of the Aradena Gorge. In which case you head left out of Anopolis until you reach the bailey bridge across the Gorge. Before this was built in the 1980s, the gift of two brothers who'd emigrated to America, the village was only reached by descending the kalderimi on one side and climbing the one on the other. A touch easier on the nerves since the wooden beams on the bridge have gaps in between, providing you with an unnerving glimpse of the bottom of the Gorge a few hundred feet below. This, however, is in its turn less nerve-shattering than being under the bridge when a car crosses above: a machine-gun-like rattling volley echoes down on you provoking an urge to dive flat.

By the time the bridge was built, Aradena was a ghost village, deserted following a series of feuds that started, apparently, from an argument over a goat bell. It has an eerie charm and there may be some renovation now taking place. There was also a kafenion on the far side – where better to have a Sfakian cheese pie (think pancake with honey)? Very soothing (until you recall you may have to re-cross the bridge)

For the round-trip you'll need to descend a kalderimi (the one on the Anopolis side is in better condition) and have two massive rockfalls to negotiate before you pick up the paths down from Livaniana. I can't recall any nightmares from the first so it must have been fairly friendly. The second, by far the biggest, was until about fifteen years ago, impossible for all but the most intrepid. Essentially, it's a sheer drop (fifty, a hundred feet? More? I daren't look), previously passable only via a rope and some iron rungs. Fortunately (Ha!) there's now a by-pass, cut high into the right-hand wall of the Gorge. Unfortunately (a) it seems to have been designed by someone who created rollercoasters since, instead of descending steadily it climbs fairly steeply and then drops down below the rockfall and (b) it was clearly built by someone about nine feet tall. This means that the steps have quite a steep drop. Not too difficult when you're climbing but as you come to the descent the drop requires you to reach down into the gap, not helping your balance, while the Gorge bottom flickers into your peripheral vision and the comforting wooden handrail proves to be a touch rickety. He'd also presumably had enough by the end as the last twenty feet or so has no steps, just a scree slope. From here it's plain sailing – till the next one.

From Anopolis the bold can, of course, head north for the mountains but it's a long trek before you get within touching distance; some guide books suggest trying for a lift from a shepherd's truck. It's also increasingly barren as you get above the tree line. OK on the nerves if you don't get lost. Even better if you don't start.

There's one other long walk from or to Loutro. The coastal walk from Agia Roumeli.

Which is the way I've always done it, preferring to be heading back home rather than aiming for, or having to wait around for, the boat. Too much for the nerves.

The 10.40 ferry from Loutro will get you to Agia Roumeli for 12. Load up with water – three litres? There's none really until Marmara – and a bit of food: there's not time for lunch unless you want a late arrival back. It's about a five-hour trek and fourteen kilometres. If lunch is an essential, doing the walk from Loutro and leaving by 10 would give you a couple of hours for a late lunch at Roumeli.

There's now a footbridge over the river to the east of Agia Roumeli and the first hour is mainly on the beach. At Agios Pavlos (taverna here if you've forgotten water) the path lifts higher and you need to watch for sharp left turns, otherwise you'll find yourself looking at uncrossable gaps above the beach. (Remember my advice in Aradena.) More walking on sand brings you to the best part of the walk – the pines, whose warm breath and scent can be wonderful, as are the views through the trees down to the sea. Somewhere along here a sign points left up to Sellouda, for Agios Ioannis and Aradena. It's always looked too steep for me and as if there's no way over the top of the cliffs, although there is, I'm told, via a kalderimi.

At the end of the pines there's a cliff with a narrow path that winds up above the sea (Don't think about it) and onto a fairly level section of about five kilometres leading to Marmara. Apart from the odd tree, there's no shade or particular feature other than the cliffs above you or the occasional passing ferry. It can seem a long stretch.

The path drops steeply down to Marmara (taverna stop permitted) and then it's another hour or so on to Loutro. A magical coastal walk, one of the best in Crete.

*

From Loutro, to the east it's two hours on foot to Sfakia. Beyond Sweetwater (invitations to join the nudists may cause some nervous sweating) you have to clamber over a section of scree and boulders about which I was once told 'Don't ever bring me across this sort of thing again.' For me, the more nerve-jangling bit is the one that follows as the path edges up round the cliff with a hundred-foot drop into the sea on your right. When you're on it it doesn't feel dangerous (though the couple of times I've done it, I've never met anyone coming down) but seeing it from the ferry brings a shudder. Once up it you're on the road down to Sfakia. On the way you'll pass the entrance to a gorge: up on the left are the faint remains of the kalderimi that cuts through the mountain (or rather the stream it follows did) up to Anopoli. You emerge into a broader shallow valley below phone masts from where it's a road walk to the Square or there's a cut through down to the Loutro path.

Given that there are plenty of ferries and taxi boats, you'll obviously only need to do the coastal walk for pleasure! From Sfakia there are a couple of trip options though any walking will have to be on road. If you've come off one of the bigger ferries, note the memorial just beyond the ramp, to the evacuation from here following the Battle.

The first trip is the Imbros Gorge. If you want to do a gorge walk but Samaria is too long and Aradena too demanding, this is the one. It is also of historical interest since in 1941 this was the route taken by the retreating Allied forces as they sought the evacuation point. You may come across a few dozen people on your way. Consider what it must have been like with twelve thousand crowding down, after a journey from Hania, perhaps largely on foot and under fire from the air. The road didn't exist then; this was the main highway south. You can also realise how the Sfakiots managed to keep their independence so long.

To walk the Gorge you first have to get to the top, which means waiting for the eleven o'clock (Hania) bus. Don't panic (more opportunities for that on the way), if it's full, another one will appear. It may also be standing room only.

After the steady climb out of Sfakia, the bus swings left by the taverna at the junction of the road with that to Frangokastello and begins the ascent of the mountain. While this comes to resemble climbing up the side of the house (and you'll realise what you've escaped by not hiring a car) the views are spectacular and the road nowadays is wider and in good condition (Probably that EU again).

Your second nervous sweat will be over where to get off. There are a couple of access points to the Gorge and the conductor or driver might call out 'Imbros!' at the first. If people pile out, you can follow, although the second stop is actually in the village of Imbros and has a larger choice of tavernas – for Sfakian cheese pie and coffee, of course. The Gorge walk is two hours, so haste isn't needed.

You're now on the Askyfou Plateau and can stay on the bus for a bit if you want, as there's a path that runs along the plateau back to Imbros. At the far end, as the road starts to climb, are signposts for a war museum (donations). Established by the present owner's father, it is more of a WW2 junk shop – his father basically just went round collecting discarded bits of Allied kit at first – and there was plenty of it, dumped in the haste to escape: fruitlessly in many cases as about six thousand were left behind when the Navy could no longer risk its ships to take off the remainder.

(You'll have to steel yourself to ask the driver to drop you here. If you find you're going downhill, you've stayed on too long. A few years ago I heard some French people in Vrysses, which is down by the National Highway and a long way from the Askyfou Plateau, ask when the next bus to the Imbros Gorge was. About two hours was the answer. Nervousness beats getting too engrossed in conversation.)

If you get off here, you'll see on a small hill ahead the crumbling remains of a Turkish fort, safely up above the surrounding countryside. They had reason to be nervous.

A fairly good path descends into the Gorge and continues steadily without any great drama or spectacular heights. There's the odd narrow section with rock arch. A kiosk part way in periodically sells entrance tickets (2€?) 'for hygienic purposes.' Some years ago, a couple of enterprising kids had set up a stall selling drinks halfway down, but they may have found easier ways to make a living since.

A peculiarity at the end of the Gorge is a couple of signs indicating 'Gorge Exit'. They actually lead into tavernas. These have obviously been set up for coach parties and if you don't want the embarrassment of walking through, continue straight on and you'll come out on the road. There may be a taxi waiting for people who don't fancy the walk back to Sfakia. Alternatively, walk up the road and through the village of Kommitades, where there are a couple of small tavernas. This road brings you to the taverna where the bus swung uphill and from here it's a downhill stroll for about three quarters of an hour into Sfakia. Note how far troops emerging from the Gorge still had to go for the chance of a boat: they were generally forced to wait here before being taken down to the beach, an attempt to bring order to the chaos.

The second trip is a bit more adventurous and has only been possible in recent years. This is a day trip to *Gavdos*, the island fifty kilometres to the south and visible from the heights above Loutro. For many years Gavdos, largely an island of exile during the twentieth century and now with a small resident population, could only be reached by infrequent ferry, mainly from Paleochora in the west. While the ferry connexion (a two-hour journey) has improved, visiting Gavdos would still involve an overnight stay, not something for the nervous since the guidebooks tended to stress the lack of water, not to mention facilities. Things have come on now, the difficulty of 'getting away from it all' driving more searchers further out and provision following.

However, the big development was the arrival of 'Gavdos Cruises', with a fast boat capable of making the crossing in an hour and so allowing about five hours on the island for a day's visit. Its departure from Sfakia at 10.15 looked nerve-wracking for anyone in Loutro because, although the big ferry leaves at 9.30 it has a habit of loitering its way to Sfakia (staff training?) and often arriving after ten. Fortunately, a new smaller ferry company now leaves Loutro earlier so the problem is reduced.

The neat arrival harbour on Gavdos, Karave (guess who funded that?), has a kafenion and shop (usually closed). A police station and town hall (deserted) on the hill above are accompanied by a scattering of other buildings. Signs of life? Little. A bus waited for day trippers who seemed to know where they were going.

I headed for Sarakiniko, described in a guide book as a forty-minute hike across the headland, though the only route appeared to be the road: tarmac and in excellent condition: the EU again, since being on the periphery of the Community gets you high status in grant applications. I can't recall actually seeing a car. It's a pleasant enough walk, through low rolling green hills with pale, sandy-looking soil.

The road peters out as it enters Sarakiniko (villages can never find the match-funding required) into a sandy dirt track that runs parallel to the beach, itself sandy and curving round a broad bay. From the beach, looking out to sea, above the distant haze, loom the peaks of the White Mountains on Crete. One taverna was open and a mini-market along a row of single storey buildings.

According to the Google map, somewhere nearby was the house occupied by Aris Velouchiotis, the famed – or notorious, depending on your political point-of-view – ELAS (Resistance) leader on mainland Greece in WW2, but it proved elusive. He was detained along with others on Gavdos in the 1930s, its providing a useful education in resistance, no doubt.

The road to Sarakiniko (name deriving from the Saracens who swarmed across the Mediterranean in Medieval times) passes a small amphitheatre/theatre set up several years ago in the hope Gavdos might become a cultural centre.

All very calm and soothing on the nerves. Less so the return journey at 5pm. I'd wondered why there were seatbelts inside the cruiser's main cabin. I found out. The wind gets up in the afternoons, making the seas rougher. As we plunged up and down the waves, I was glad I'd made my will. It was, of course, no storm, just a bit of swell, but for the nervous traveller... My friend Rob Innis would have loved it.

*

EAST FROM SFAKIA

As indicated earlier, going east from Sfakia means by road. A few years ago there was a minibus that ran to Frangokastello, about twenty minutes away but I'm not sure if it still runs. For several years I made the journey to Rodakino, my next destination, on foot, about six hours in all.

With a pack weighing about forty pounds, the long slog up to the taverna near Kommitades was hard-going. I could have waited for the 11 o'clock bus but I was virtually at the top before it passed me. The first time I did it I'd thought of getting a taxi but couldn't see any (there's a good taxi office in the supermarket on the harbour front) so irritation drove me on. From Kommitades, through a series of small villages, the going is fairly level, if not particularly entrancing. The road passes some way inland from Frangokastello, a small resort with one of the most modern Byzantine castles you'll meet (thanks to Arthur Evans' example) and just past the second turning there's a minor road going straight on that cuts off a winding, uphill chunk of the main road to Rodakino, becomes a dirt road and comes out on the long beach below the village. From here to the Polyrizos Hotel (my destination) it's less than an hour. Easy on the nerves unless you're running out of water.

But let's approach on the main road. Rodakino is either one village split by a ravine or two villages, Ano (Upper) Rodakino and Kato (Lower) Rodakino divided by the same ravine. We're high up now, closer to the mountain range on the left and some way above the sea. Ano Rodakino straggles along the road as it winds round and down across the ravine, a new bridge on a wide curving bend posing far fewer problems for the nervous driver than the narrow bends down to the old stone humped bridge ever did.

Kato Rodakino is the larger settlement, spreading out down the hill a little. For spectacle both are really best approached from the opposite direction since, as you swing round the headland, you're confronted by the great gash of the ravine in the mountain below which they sit. Canyoning is popular… you must be joking.

From Kato Rodakino a road runs down a couple of kilometres to the beach, with a sprinkling of holiday properties to your left, together with a taverna and trendy bar. This is Koraka beach which The Rough Guide continues to insist is from where the kidnapped German General Kreipe was taken off the island in 1944 by Patrick Leigh Fermor, Billy Moss and their Cretan associates. However, the Cretan historian Giorgos Harokopos from Patsos near Spili, who as a lad joined the abductors, says in his book 'The Abduction of General Kreipe' that it was Peristeres beach, further west, so he should know.

At Koraka beach the road swings west, reaching in a kilometre or so Polirizos beach with the excellent Nikos and Anna Taverna, now run by their son. The village supermarket has also relocated down here and there's another taverna and a bar. The road then turns uphill, passing the Polyrizos Hotel, with a branch off down to Peristeres beach (a recent development once the farm sold out for holiday villas), before winding, narrowing and climbing steeply to reach the main road west of Ano Rodakino. Not recommended for the faint-hearted driver.

But back to the Polyrizos Hotel. The Rough Guide describes it as 'relatively large and fancy' though, as it's a series of white cubes set among the olive groves, it doesn't feel large; nor does 'fancy' catch the simplicity of the design or the restrained comfort of the interiors. Run by brothers Markos and Nikos and their wives, when Grandma did the cooking it was the best in Crete; now she supervises to keep up the standard. She, incidentally, saw the General as he was brought through in 1944.

Until a few years ago the 'secret' beach of Peristeres was only accessible by crossing the headland on a path that starts in the left-hand corner of the Anna and Nikos taverna car park. This still exists, but the descent to the beach is slightly more difficult as the direct access is fenced off. The beach was deserted then, apart from a small chapel at the far end, though now there's also a kafenion at each end.

From the Poliziros there's a circular walk, turning right outside the entrance and following the road as it winds up to the main road, then taking that through the villages and down again to the beach. As you climb, the capes unfold to the east, though the view is equally impressive from the terrace of the Anna and Nikos taverna.

The two mountains above the villages were once accessible, the round-topped one probably still the case, starting from Ano Rodakino though, when I went up, I was startled near the top by a cavalcade of motor-cyclists coming down, presumably having driven from the other side. The higher (4000 feet) and more craggy one, Krioneritis, with a path starting off the main road near the edge of Kato Rodakino, is almost inaccessible now, the path above the village being overgrown. If you get beyond there (and it may be necessary to follow the road up and round the headland before taking a track uphill to do so) a dirt road ascends past some masts to the summit. It is, however, a long drag and I never made it over the summit to see what there was to the north.

A more rewarding walk is the coastal one to Plakias, about two and a half hours to the east. To return you either have to come back the same way or get a taxi. At the Koraka end of the beach there's a short, steep ascent to take you above the sea, revealing a small harbour below and the Akropoli Rooms ahead, stuck on an outcrop of rock high above the water. A wide track winds and climbs its way round the headlands before dropping down, after nearly two hours, to Souda and the coast road into Plakias.

One warning for the nervous, though it may now be better. Traditionally, shepherds would stay with their flocks up in the hills for the summer. This was partly to stop them wandering off – or being stolen – since until it joined the EU Greece had no land registry and therefore not much need for fences. Nowadays metal fences proliferate and a shepherd will generally just drive up in his pickup periodically to feed/check on his flock. Hence also the growth of dirt roads across the landscape. The fences, of course, need a gate to let traffic through: it's usually just a section of the metal fencing that will swing open (The first time I came across one I thought there was no opening) when unfastened.

This contrivance is, however, an inconvenience for the driver: he has to stop, get out, open the gate, get back in etc. Far too much trouble. The answer? Remove the gate section, tie a length of wire on the ground across the gap and attach a dog to it by its chain. Because the dog can roam across the gap it can effectively block the egress of any sheep. Or human. Given that the dog is (a) bored stiff because it hasn't seen a sheep in days (b) half-crazed, starved and parched by the sun, its performance of its duties is usually done with a good deal of aggression. Especially to humans.

At one stage there were two of these obstacles on the way to Plakias. The first I came to on a narrow section just past the Akrotiri, with a high bank to one side and a steep drop to the other. No way round. Fortunately, Grandma had given me a bag of homemade biscuits before I left and, by lobbing one to the dog at one side of the gap, I was able (just) to nip across the other side. It was a close-run thing. At the second gate the dog was quick to grab the biscuit in mid-air and simultaneously swing back before I could cross. It needed a second, placed less close to it, before I could effect my escape.

As I was not returning but going on from Plakias, I didn't have to repeat the exercise later and the last time I did the route the gates were unattended (the shepherd had probably sold the sheep and opened a bar) but a packet of biscuits might be advised if you contemplate the walk (doctored steak a la Sherlock Holmes is too difficult to acquire down there). Nerves don't come into it.

In the last thirty years Plakias has grown into a fairly substantial resort, spreading both east and west along the coast, although the centre of the original village retains its low-key origins. There were pleasant walks into the hinterland and up to the villages of Sellia and Myrthios in the hills. An excellent hand-drawn map by Lance Chilton is/ was available in local supermarkets.

Walking along the coast east of Plakias isn't really practical. At the far end of the long curving beach (careful, I'm told there's a nudist section there) a tunnel enters the headland: former German coastal defences. I once saw some people go in but never saw them come out. (You obviously wouldn't consider it either).

To reach Preveli, about ten kilometres east of Plakias, involves a road walk or bus, but it is a bit of a diversion off the bus route heading north to Rethymnon. Preveli's main claim to fame is the monastery, which played a leading role in getting stranded troops off the island in 1941 after the Battle. Nowadays more people probably head for the beach below with its palm trees.

To travel east, the main road – the Rethymnon-Agia Galini road – runs a long way inland and to reach the south coast before Galini requires a car, or a long road walk. But on the way the main road goes through Spili. We're now in Central Crete.

CENTRAL CRETE

SPILI

Nestling in an elevated position below Spili Mountain, the town/large village is midway between Rethymnon in the north and Agia Galini on the south coast. A working town though now much given to passing tourism, its main attraction is a row of once-Venetian lion-headed fountains above the square, from which the deliciously cool water flows unceasingly. The current lion faces are probably at least the third generation and recent 'improvements' to the site included removing the stone slab at the entrance, which carried the text of Cavafy's poem 'Thermopylae'. It was never that clear what link Thermopylae had to Spili, though maybe the poem's ending presaged the slab's fate.

The petrol pumps that once stood on the right-angle bend at the centre of the town have also now gone. (Touch of relief for the nervous: less chance of a conflagration) Yianni's taverna just up from the bend has excellent Cretan food and wine, while on the way to it you'll pass the Merival shop, full of locally-produced soaps and other natural products, many grown by Stephano in what he calls his 'garden' on the way into the village. Korres may have cornered the international market but Stephano's products are excellent. He also runs the Green Hotel, with views across the valley, although most of his time is now devoted to the garden and shop.

Once the coach parties have gone Spili remains a low-key place but a good example of a 'real' Cretan town, with raki from the barrel at the shop opposite Yianni's. When I went in without a bottle, the shopkeeper took a small bottle of water, threw the contents out into the road and filled up. No extra charge. An intriguing short walk is up the Spili Gorge, though it's really more of a gap in the hill and shouldn't frighten the nervous. Going up the path to the right of the fountains you come to a gate/old bedstead in the fence on your left and opening this is likely to be the main stress. A path then winds up the hill, with fine views over the valley, until it climbs over the rocks at the top and then descends through the trees to the chapel of Agia Pnevma, a comparatively new construction below the main road to Yerakari. A track curves round the valley beyond the chapel but of the path that presumably once led up and towards Yerakari there's now no trace. Descending the main road, you'll come to a track that leads down through the upper part of the village and back to the square.

There are several longer walks possible from Spili (see the Rough Guide), though most involve mainly road sections. Having said that, going south by road to Mourne and then down to the right to Frati (not a very clear section through woods, oops, nerve alert) will bring you back along a pleasantly-wooded valley to Mixourima and the main road back to Spili.

If you're travelling by bus, your main worry, since the timetables don't give times for intermediate stops, will be whether you'll miss the onward one. While noting how long it took to get there can be a guide (and each direction is about half an hour away), it can't be relied on – the driver might be in a hurry or on the other hand need to stop, as I once saw, for a wee on the way. Allow yourself ten minutes to ease the worry and accept the wait – it'll probably turn up ten minutes late anyway: not relaxing if you've got a connexion in Rethymnon. There was a time when the bus from Spili would make it to the outskirts of Rethymnon with a good ten minutes to spare – then get stuck in traffic. To avoid this, it often goes left along the National Highway and enters the town from the west, so avoiding the major snarl-ups. However, another way of facilitating connexions has been to start the bus from Galini a quarter of an hour earlier. If you've not been able to pick up a printed timetable in Rethymnon, this could scupper your elaborate schemes to catch the bus.

Obviously, all this could be enough to deter you from Spili for life, but, come on. Live on the edge a little. It'll be worth it. OK, hire a car. Though I did warn you…

By continuing south from Spili with a car, you can divert via Saktouria to Agios Pavlos, an out-the-way place near the beach. A German once told me that it was the best place in Crete; perhaps if you want no-key but I prefer the slightly more signs-of-life in Loutro.

Agia Galini, at the end of the road, is the first place I stayed in on Crete so has a lot to answer for. In 1982 it was not much more than Taverna Street, running down to a broad quay (now a car park) on which you could breakfast. Being wedged into a narrow cleft in the hills, development has not been over-obtrusive. From the bars above the harbour, you could look east to Matala and Festos and muse, over an ouzo, on the birth of civilisation. Far easier on the nerves than musing on its end.

A pleasant 4km walk from Galini is to the west and Agios Giorgios, along a fairly clear track/path. A quaint outdoor kantina off the main road provided lunch, including homemade fava.

From Galini you can visit Festos, one of the main Minoan sites which, although not partially reconstructed like Knossos, has a dramatic setting between mountains and sea. But from here it's back up to the north coast and Rethymnon.

The third largest city in Crete, Rethymnon, midway between Chania and Heraklion, suffers somewhat by comparison. Lacking the sweep of Chania's harbour and with a smaller old town, it does nevertheless have some understated attractions, though its tourist accommodation stretches a long way to the east. It's one of those places where, if you're booking a package, you need to establish exactly how far the hotel is from the centre. During the Battle in 1941 the German paratroop landings here were an almost complete failure. However, the successful Allied forces (mainly Australian) then found that they were cut off from the main evacuation route further west.

If you walk up the steps at the back of the bus station (now refurbished so no longer quite the reminder that the word 'chaos' is Greek, but still suffering from its cramped location) to the main road and turn left, you'll come to a small park containing the Australian War Memorial. Pleasant shade. And soothing for the nerves.

From Rethymnon the new National Highway sweeps up and down the coastal hills, the terrain always interesting and often dramatic. (the Old Road lies further inland to the south and passes through Anoigia, scene of a massacre during the war, supposedly in retaliation for the kidnap of General Kreipe though as it took place some months later the motivation may have just been mindless hate) Next is

HERAKLION

The capital. Not as immediately captivating as Hania, Heraklion probably has more sites of interest, both in itself and nearby. Central to these is the Archaeological Museum, recently refurbished and rightly regarded as the foremost museum of Minoan civilisation anywhere in the world. The quality and detail of its exhibits are breath-taking, while the sheer quantity may require a lie down. When I last visited, the café was closed, which didn't help the mind to unboggle.

However, the Historical Museum doesn't lag far behind with some excellent features, including a room detailing the long siege of the town by the Turks before it finally fell and a mock-up of the study of Nikos Kazantzakis ('Zorba the Greek').

Kazantzakis, who was born to the south of Heraklion and whose father's house now hosts a museum, is buried on the walls of the city: walk through the market, veer rightwards a bit at the square beyond and keep going until you see a stadium; it's next door – a plain wooden cross, a rough low stone slab and an inscription 'I expect nothing, I fear nothing, I am free'. With the sea visible to the north across the roofs of the city, your nerves would be settled if you were buried there.

Time for a digression about Kazantzakis. Though known in the UK mainly though Zorba (and the film at that; the book, a vibrant celebration of life, is neglected but well worth reading. The film, incidentally, despite becoming an international success, lasted only a week in Hania as the locals hated its unsentimental portrayal of village life), several of his other books deserve attention. The novel 'Freedom and Death' recounts events during the Turkish occupation and provides a sharp picture of the refusal of Cretans to be bowed by the frequent inhumanity of the Turks. As a Cretan in those days your nerves would have been permanently on edge, or chopped off. The autobiographical essays in 'Report to Greco' set out his philosophy – 'always take the road that ascends' – and his memorable assertion 'Crete expands the soul'. Even less well known is that fact that he once came to the UK, in 1939, and produced a book – 'England' – about the trip, though the heavy industry areas of Birmingham and Manchester seemed to him like the circles of Hell.

Back to Heraklion.

You can then walk from the Kazantzakis tomb along the walls down towards the sea, although the walls don't extend that far. The seafront west of the harbour underwent considerable development of bars and restaurants for the Olympics, while the harbour itself features a Venetian castle.

The city has a lively feel, not only dependent on tourism for its buzz.

The major Minoan site on the island, Knossos, lies a few miles to the south. It's become something of a theme park, very crowded and with several rooms only able to be looked into rather than visited. Local blue and white buses (No 2?) start from next to the old main bus station along from the harbour.

Another intriguing site to the south is Arkhanes, a twenty-minute ride on a green bus (from the new bus station, up the road from the old one and with a good café). It has an interesting museum but is also the start of the climb up Mount Yiouktas, the jagged peak you can see from Heraklion. A path (it's not very clear where it starts, find a German with a guidebook) zigzags up the hill, from where the views are spectacular. Not far off is Anemospilia where indications of human sacrifice were found not long ago. (No, don't panic, it's the discovery that was not long ago, the remains were Minoan.)

The airport is a ten-minute bus ride from the centre (No 1 bus from the main square, tickets from a machine: bit of a panic opportunity, choose purple) so staying in the city is convenient. The Hotel Daedelos on the pedestrianised Daedelou Street was a good bet, although it was closed for several years for refurbishment and may have gone upmarket since. The Hotel El Greco, not far from the market, is a good alternative. With either, you're not wandering around the back streets in the dark. (Incidentally, if you're catching the bus *from* the airport – turn left out of the perimeter fence – there's a kiosk selling tickets. Another tip, if I haven't mentioned it already: hold your ticket out to the driver so he can tear off half. Technology hasn't arrived yet, with machines to cancel the tickets).

The coastal strip east of Heraklion was the earliest to be developed on Crete and has continued so, heavily. Not until you pass Malia ('the town that never sleeps') do you leave mass tourism behind and then only for a while. We're now in

EASTERN CRETE

And the first major town, Agios Nicholaos, another early-developed resort although it has retained more of its character than other places, largely by going upmarket in the past thirty years. The bus station, moved and refurbished a few years ago, is now up the hill on the edge of town, useful for avoiding traffic snarl-ups if you're going east or west. Venturing down into the town is fairly clear though finding your way back up could stretch the nerves. When you reach a roundabout, turn left.

And good news for the nervous bladder, er traveller: bus station refurbishment includes the toilets which, at Rethymnon and Heraklion especially, previously left a lot to be desired, like locks, seats. Clearly this once-in-a-lifetime refurbishment means that the more recent jobs, like Heraklion, are likely to retain their new splendour longer. Agios, which was one of the first to be done, is already showing signs of wear – but still very serviceable, never fear. (I'm glad that's one worry ameliorated.)

Now spreading round the Bay of Mirabello, Agios Nicholaos to the north and over a steep hill, leads to Elounda, a resort town that now itself stretches along the coast up towards Plaka, across the water from the former leper colony,

Spinalonga. As with Rethymnon, if you're booking a hotel here, it's worth finding out exactly where it is in relation to the centre.

The descent into Elounda provides dramatic views over the bay, the near side being the location of several very upmarket hotels that do little for the local economy and in which you could be anywhere in the world. On the way in, just as the village starts, you'll pass on the left the Thea Taverna, run by Manolis, born in Plaka and whose mother (after whom the taverna is named), when a girl, remembered being taken by boat to anchor off the island and sing to the inhabitants on festival days. Across from the Thea and along a path is the good Hotel Akti Olous, on the causeway.

(Although there are plenty of rooms in Elounda, most are assigned to package holiday companies and owners are reluctant to let out anything for a day or two's stay. Didn't do my temper – forget the nerves – much good tramping round looking for somewhere)

Elounda's popularity has grown in recent years because of the novel, 'The Island', which exploited the leper island's history and also became a highly-regarded Greek TV series. (The book's first sentence – 'A cold wind whipped through the narrow streets of Plaka' – always clashed with my memory and, when I next saw Manolis, I asked him how many streets there were in Plaka. His answer – 'one' – echoed my recollection, though recent developments probably mean the book is now right)

Boat trips to the island leave from both Elounda and Plaka and you get an hour there instead of the half hour years ago. This is partly because in the past there were only the abandoned houses to see; now some have been refurbished and host exhibits and displays showing the history. Progress, I suppose, from when you gave a few hundred drachma to an English-speaking guide for the same, but knowledge has come at the expense of the melancholic atmosphere that still lingered then. There is at least easily enough time to do a circuit of the island in addition to looking at the exhibitions. Again, you'll be worrying about missing the boat back, especially as there are often so many with few distinguishing features. If you're going back to Plaka, it doesn't seem to matter, you just get on any that calls out 'Plaka'.

From the causeway there is an interesting walk over the actual Spinalonga, the long spine which encloses the bay in front of Elounda, even if the paths are faint.

Inland from and to the west of Agios Nicholaos is the large village of Kritsa, a pleasant place with small gorge that makes interesting walking, and nearby is the archaeological site of Lato. All worth a diversion by bus from Agios.

Travelling east, development continues, though in a fairly low-rise fashion, to Istro, after which the bends in the road and difficult access to the sea have restricted building. However, in Minoan times the small town of Gournia was founded here, its excavation easily accessible from the main road and enabling a clear view of the layout. It's not the only clear view, as before you looms the great wall of the Sitia mountains.

There are a few places worth a stop from here on to Sitia, a couple of hours further by bus. Pacchia Ammos has rooms and tavernas on the beach and good views up the Gulf of Mirabello, although the locals have had to erect a barrier across the harbour and beachfront to catch the rubbish that floats down on the wind. Walks in the hinterland of olive groves lead, as so often in this part of Crete, to a Minoan site, in this case Vassiliki, unassuming but a delight to stumble on. However, an attempt to go up Thripti was thwarted by E4 footpath signs that seemed to lead nowhere fast.

Beyond Pacchia Ammos and the turn south to Ierapetra, the road ascends steadily along the side of the Gulf, with masses of oleander lining the way. Kavousi, towards the top of the hill, has a good roadside taverna and rooms – as a sign of the times, I'd be eating the excellent traditional fare and the local kids would come in for crisps or beefburgers. From the village, paths and tracks lead up to the scattered village of Thripti, in fact so scattered I never managed to find it. The information board on the main road had useful direction points like 'turn left near the ancient olive tree', the only problem being there seemed to be about ten thousand of them.

As with Spili, if you're travelling onward by bus from here or Pacchia Ammos, the challenge is to estimate how long it will take it to arrive from Sitia (and where it stops, since there are no signs). Once more, noting on the way in is the only vague help, with probably more of a wait on the roadside, nerves jangling.

Further on, there are two turnings for Mochlos (take the second), a small village by the sea and with an archaeological site on the island just opposite. Another low-key place, out-of-the-way because it is accessible really only by car.

The road then winds up and down and round, the bus turning off periodically to visit interesting little villages perched on top of adjacent hills (often to deliver postal packages, all part of the service), though as it approaches Sitia a new road involving high-level bridges (the EU again) straightens things out as it descends.

SITIA

The main town in this area of north-eastern Crete, Sitia, lying against the hillside and overlooking a wide bay, has a welcoming aspect. A working town, mainly serving its agricultural hinterland, its two streets of small shops, running across the hill and parallel to the waterfront, have a profusion of local produce, from land and sea. An excellent small museum has some intriguing exhibits. A circular walk of a few hours, starting east along the main road and then up to Roussa Eklissia, across to Episkopi and back via the main road, will probably take in as many Minoan sites in that time, most simply individual villas or farms, as you'll have come across in the past several years. In Minoan times there was a profusion of everyday life here besides the major palace settlements.

Somebody clearly had designs on turning this area of Crete into a major tourist destination. The airport has a runway capable of taking international flights but so far remains unexploited – fortunately, since mass tourism would destroy the ethos of the place, as it has in many areas west. Other signs of this ambition are the skeletal concrete frame of a hotel that has never progressed beyond that stage, a strange, Portmeirion-like development on the road to Palekastro, deserted now by the look of it, and the road beyond, widened to resemble another airport runway. The latter may be related to a scheme for a mega development on the coast involving golf courses and luxury hotels that luckily failed to get planning permission. Don't breathe a sigh of relief too soon. (As if you would). They'll be back with bigger bribes.

Such a development would clearly also destroy the charm of Palekastro, the most-easterly town in Crete. Serving its agricultural heartland, its small central square hosts a few tavernas and the excellent Hotel Hellas (also with great food).

From the centre a road leads through olive groves for a couple of kilometres to the beach and the Minoan town of Palekastro, its main street still traversable and notable for the tranquillity of its setting. Your nerves will be deservedly relaxing here.

It's possible to stroll on tracks along the bay, through the olive groves, even venturing up the flat-topped hill that overlooks the beach, or climbing the path inland to the Peak Sanctuary. A longer but easy road walk (2 hours) will take you to Vai, the vaunted Palm Beach or on to the more interesting site of Itanos, yet another long-lost city of antiquity, though compared to Palekastro there's not much to see.

It is possible to walk by a track over the hills (and under the wind farms) to Sitia, coming out at Roussa Eklissia, though – a warning for the nervous – if you do it on a day when shooting is permitted – Sunday and Thursday? Sorry, no help – it can be a bit worrying to see, or hear, which is worse, blokes with rifles wandering about.

A major attraction in this area is the Minoan Palace site of Kato Zakros. Owing to the fact that the only bus via Palekastro now departs at 6am, it really needs a car – or taxi if you can find one. As you round the headland above the bay at Kato Zakros, a dramatic picture unfolds before you, of the beach backed by looming mountains. But if you're driving, be alert, goats often decide to sunbathe on the road at the top.

The site was only discovered in the 1960s and so, though small, its layout remains fairly intact and the place is easy to wander around.

Kato Zakros is, however, one of those places where, if you're a single (let alone, nervous) traveller, people are reluctant to give you a room for the night because a couple might turn up later and be able to be charged a few euros more. I hadn't thought of shouting 'Just charge me the bloody room rate' in those days, being more price conscious. With a car I went back past the headland and followed signs down a track for Alex Rooms. Quaint accommodation rather like a cell with the only window in the door, but a modern shower block. Nerves – and irritation – calmed.

On another occasion, on foot (there must have been a mid-morning bus at that time) I got fed up and stumped up the Gorge of the Dead (no, don't panic, the name comes from the caves high up in the walls that were, apparently, used as Minoan burial chambers. They aren't still looking for victims). The gorge itself isn't deep and it's merely a gradual two hour trek up to Ano (Upper) Zakros.

Where I stayed at the Hotel Zakros, then, that is c2005, an unreconstructed 1960s place with a slightly Gothic feel, the net curtains of the same vintage harbouring some giant spider. It wasn't quite like the motel in 'Psycho' but I won't stress your nerves by recommending it (Unless you're a Goth). The nearby Napoleon taverna, however, was excellent, even if the name seems a bit unlikely for this part of the world. (But see later in Ierapetra).

The Hotel Zakros had a final sting. As I was paying (18€ per night) the old dear running the place struggled to count out my four euros change in fifty cent coins while carrying on a conversation on the phone with her daughter. I merely lost the will to live and became catatonic while waiting. Unfortunate, as you'll see.

I was heading back to Palekastro, a mainly road trip though with a track cutting off a long loop of the road. A few hours at most. Rain had been skirting about the previous day but the weather looked as if it might hold. Pausing only for a few words with an Austrian I'd seen the day before, I set off, keeping a wary eye on the clouds.

About three quarters of an hour out, for some reason I touched the pocket where my passport was. Or wasn't. Then I realised. In the confusion of giving me my change the old dear had forgotten to return my passport. And I was too bemused to notice.

So back it was. Profuse apologies and off again. Only an hour and a half behind schedule. But who was worrying about a schedule? What could cause stress?

The rain? It began when I was about an hour and a half from Palekastro. And grew in intensity. I had a cagoule but decided that I'd get as wet from inside as from the rain. By the time I reached Palekastro the roads were awash and apart from a corner of my wallet I was completely soaked. The contents of the rucksac were dry, long-established worry about their getting wet having meant they were in plastic bags.

The benefits, well, one, of being a nervous traveller!

So I staggered back to the Hotel Hellas for two days while my walking shoes dried out. Not much of a hardship and no strain on the nerves once inside.

Leaving Palekastro by bus induces similar anxiety to that mentioned earlier at Spili and other places, though the bus only has to come from Vai. As there are usually a number of people waiting, some comfort can be derived from the crowd. The last time I made the journey I was due to make a connexion in Sitia for Ierapetra, but was fairly relaxed (No, really) as there was plenty of time for the transfer. Of course, the bus was late coming. Still no problem as it reached the village before Sitia at 12.20: the connexion was 12.30. Should be OK. Nerves a bit taut but not jangling. Then the bus pulled into a school car park and waited while the kids faffed about saying goodbye to their friends before getting on. Arrival at Sitia Bus station 12.32.

Was I panicking? Fuming? No, just despairing. Then I realised that the driver was changing the sign on the bus I'd arrived on: to Ierapetra. Quick dash to buy ticket. Clue as to why he had been dawdling. And lesson about worrying too soon.

I'd never stayed in Ierapetra before, only passed through its bus station on the way to Myrtos to the west. Nor had I travelled on this bus route though when we reached the south coast the bus went through Makriyialos, a place I'd stayed in in October for several years running until whatever now-defunct travel company decided it no longer wanted single travellers, even with their supplement.

(A note on single supplements, something you **can** get agitated about. Travel companies usually try to blame the accommodation owners but since the companies merely block book a given number of rooms for a flat rate (and a low one at that, from what a rep told me once in Elounda) it's their profit that suffers if there's only one person occupying the room, not two. If you're travelling independently, you'll either just pay the room rate or actually get a discount for one person. Following the economic crisis in Greece, I suspect the former will become the norm. Fair enough, at least you're not charged extra for taking up no more space.)

Makriyialos seems a nondescript place as you pass by since most of its buildings front onto the long beach (which is what the name means), with their backs to the road. A sandy beach with relatively shallow water beyond and good food, what more could you want? Well, there's an agreeable walk up into the hills via the Pefki Gorge (no, it's not frightening either) to the village of Pefki, with a pleasant taverna. It was in Makriyialos I first came across pitta gyros (kebab to you), the Greek contribution to a fast-food lunch. Ask for all the fillings: chips, yoghurt, onion, tomato as well as the pork slices. Great for everything, including the nerves.

Ierapetra tends to be dismissed by the critical as lacking character but it has a warm feel, and not only because it, apparently, has the most hours of sunshine in Crete. It is also claimed to be the southernmost town (or city, since the Greek words are the same) in Europe. I think somewhere in Cyprus might dispute the claim but Ierapetra is south of some parts of north west Africa.

It sprawls along a wide beach with plenty of places to laze with a coffee. Or have sardines for lunch beside the sea. I stayed in the Hotel El Greco, sea-facing room with glorious views and an excellent breakfast choice.

There's not much to see in Ierapetra: a small archaeological museum housed in a former Turkish school has some interesting bits and pieces while the castle (blocked off for renovations when I was there) is little more than a shell. However, there is Napoleon's House!

As indicated above at the Ano Zakros taverna, it's not the most obvious place in the world to come across Napoleon. Until you recall that he did have ambitions to become a pharaoh in Egypt. Nelson put an end to these hopes at the

Battle of the Nile and he had to make a swift exit. Possibly via Ierapetra.

Whether he stayed for one night on his way to Egypt or on the way back, fleeing from the British fleet, is not entirely clear. Nevertheless, the house where he reputedly lodged is signposted from several directions. Leading you to a small, two-storey end terrace identifiable as the august dwelling by a sheet of white A4 paper bearing the typed words 'Napoleon's House' pinned to the door. The windows were shuttered and padlock on the door looked as if it might not have been opened since 1798. A tourist attraction unexploited though, as at the museum, where I was the only one around that month, not necessarily surprisingly.

Virtually everywhere in Ierapetra seemed to be advertising boat trips to Krissi island, ten kilometres to the south. Looked intriguing. Next time, certainly.

My previous visit to Ierapetra bus station (and it's barely that, more of a shop front on a layby) had been to get the bus a few miles west to Myrtos, a small resort off the main road, beside the sea. From Myrtos there are walks inland up the valley or along the coast to the west. Nothing spectacular although I remember a taverna (at Tertsa) where the owner tried the old trick of claiming it was a five thousand drachma note I'd given him, and not the ten thousand I actually had. He gave in eventually.

Driving further west the road turns north to Kastelli, projected site of a replacement airport for Heraklion, though the crisis may have put paid to this also. When I moaned to Stephano in Spili about how far from Heraklion this would be, he pointed out that, because the airport there was next to the sea, it was exposed to the north winds and on occasions planes were turned back to Athens because of this.

So Crete 'done' and your nerves still intact? Don't worry, the adventure's only just starting. There'll be plenty more opportunities to test the nerves. Next is the chain known as the Dodecanese (twelve islands – or thereabouts!) Of which the first is Karpathos.

KARPATHOS

A long thin spine of rock midway between Crete and Rhodes, Karpathos was until recently an island of two halves, the more developed south with the capital, Pigardia, and the remoter north, largely cut off by land until the tarmac road was finally completed around 2015.

(The inability to finish the road may not have been entirely due to the depradations of nature, which each winter appeared to wash away the work done in the summer on the last section close to Olymbos. Prior to the road's completion, travel to the north was largely restricted to 4x4s, since car hire companies forbade travel on the unmade section and taxis used to charge a hundred euros there from the airport. Transport from the south was therefore by boat to the northern port of Diafani.)

There was a community boat that made the hour-long trip two or three times a week but also the tourist boats taking people via Diafani to the traditional village of Olymbos, a few miles on the other side of the island. Clearly the road will have affected that business and it can't be long before a coach does the trip from Pigardia anyway. Which would be a shame because, although the road is scenic, the boat trip offers dramatic views of the island's spine, besides the possibility of seeing a dolphin dive under the prow. The growth in vehicle traffic won't help either. As for the community boat, the economic crisis had put an end to that, so perhaps the successful road-building became a necessity.

I first came to Karpathos in 2005 as a result of seeing a photo or postcard of Olymbos, the so-called traditional village clinging vertiginously to the side of a mountain. In the sun. (More of that later). It looked scintillating.

In those days I used to come by ferry from Crete, since I'd been able to arrive there earlier the same day and avoid an overnight stay. At 10pm, therefore, I was in Sitia, waiting for the boat and having avoided the stress of worrying if they'd sell tickets on the quay (they did), by buying one earlier from a travel agent.

I hadn't realised then that an hour's delay could be the norm, depending on how many stops the ship had made on its trip from Piraeus and how much lorry traffic needed to be loaded or unloaded. From Sitia the journey takes about the same time – five hours – as from Rhodes. (Add two hours if coming from Heraklion and another one if going on to Diafani). At 3am therefore, rather than 2am – what was I thinking of even to attempt it? – I found myself standing on the vast, dark, empty quay at Pigardia, as the other three disembarkees disappeared into the night.

A solitary car was parked near the entrance to the quay and as I approached a man got out and asked if I wanted a room. What can you say? Maybe I hadn't become a nervous traveller then. Or, more likely, I was too jet-lagged to notice. Making clear I wanted something in the town and being told it was just up the hill, I got in. As the car shot off along the flat, the driver explained that the one-way system meant the road zigzagged to get there. It wasn't cheap, 35€ a night (remember the 18 at Ano Zakros?), but at 3am in the middle of nowhere, who's going to argue? Certainly not even a pre-nervous traveller (Pre-? Is that amnesia?). Besides, it was actually an apartment and easily far better than the18€ job.

Pigardia, the capital, is an amenable place, not traditionally that given up to tourism (the wealth of returned Australian emigrants providing sustenance enough) although in recent years some large, ugly hotels have been erected along the beach. Being unable to locate a bus station (the single bus probably being off somewhere and no other evidence of one visible), I walked inland for a few hours but didn't get as far as the other side of the island where there are a few resorts, not far from the airport. (During the Battle of Crete this airport, the island as with all the Dodecanese being Italian-controlled, was the base used to bomb ships evacuating the garrison from Heraklion, as they negotiated the Kassos Channel to the east of Crete, on their flight to Egypt. Several never made it. The island was then known as Scarpanto).

Next day it was the tourist boat up the coast, then an ancient German coach along the winding road to Olymbos with photo stop on the way. Olymbos does look dramatic, coloured houses clinging to the side of the hill, especially in the sun (I am coming to that). Although to a degree now a marketing ploy, the isolation of Olymbos meant it retained traditional elements long after most other places had lost them. The women still wear traditional, multi-coloured costumes (and don't seem to ditch them as soon as the tourists have left).

The streets of Olymbos are too narrow for traffic so it's all on foot from the car park. I made the mistake of accepting the offer of a room not far along the way: my general line is to refuse offers until I've had a chance to look around but, of course, I often forget – or am worried I might not find anywhere. Mistake because the room was fairly basic and if I'd hung on, I might have hit the Hotel Aphrodite, on the edge of the village with sensational views down the coast (see front cover) and with breakfast for the same price I was paying (without breakfast, sea view, hot water or much toilet paper – but no problem with the last: the nervous traveller always carries spare). I learnt this (the hotel) from an Austrian I met on a walk, who'd also got a direct flight from his country. No such luck for Brits, though on the other hand the absence of flights may be a bonus. A few years ago, the Times did a big travel feature about Karpathos and the next time I arrived I was concerned it might be over-run. Result? Fewer than previously. Too down-market for Times readers? We can only hope so.

Incidentally, the Austrian did say that it was so windy at his hotel that the shutters rattled: maybe it wouldn't have been good for my nerves after all.

There were two benefits from my mistake. One was that the old lady next door just up the hill gave me a bunch of grapes and two bunches of dried thyme. Her main expression (I didn't speak much Greek in those days) was 'aera' (wind). Hmm. The other was a balcony view of a wedding procession. The groom, from Diafani was coming to marry a girl in the village and, as the cars could come no nearer the church than the car park, the groom's procession had to pass below my room. It was a raucous affair, with band and guns being fired.

Two things stood out. The first was the groom, who appeared to be carried along by a man either side, so that he resembled a mafiosi victim being led to execution.

Maybe he was. Certainly a nervous groom. (Further guidebook opportunity?)

The second notable event – for me – was that as the procession passed, two men firing rifles into the air brought up the rear. After they'd gone, a pigeon suddenly flopped down onto the now-empty street, blood seeping from under it. I wondered if this was an omen. Sometime later when I looked out, probably anxious in case I'd have to step over it, it had gone. That calmed *my* nerves.

Naturally the Austrian had been invited to the wedding. I missed out.

Once the tourists depart in the early afternoon for some beach time in Diafani before the boat back south, the village becomes deserted. And when the sun's gone, grim. The surrounding hillsides are of a bare, grey rock and with no sun on them the place is reminiscent of a Welsh slate quarry village. But there are plenty of walks.

The first walk I tried was down to the beach, Fysses, 300 metres below, on a path mentioned in 'The Rough Guide to the Greek Islands'. The path wasn't that clear and as I descended further had been cut off by a dirt road whose destination wasn't clear either. About twenty metres above the shore any further progress seemed to end. It clearly wasn't a bathing spot, though on the excellent ROAD map it had an umbrella. I trudged back up.

There is a path leading south from the village, below the ruined windmills, high above the sea. Some way along is a turning up Profitas Ilias, the mountain that guards/looms over Olymbos. I resisted the temptation (lack of time, not nerve, ha, ha, ha). The coastal path came out on the road, where work was still continuing, as it would for a decade, to make the link from the south. Again, I returned.

More profitable are the walks to the north of Olymbos. The principal route drops sharply out of the village, down the steps beside the taverna by the windmill and up the valley, cutting off the wide bend the road from Diafani has to take. One track heads straight up the valley, over the hill and down to Avlona, a scattered hamlet (plus taverna) with a sporadic population. From there paths lead on to Vrougounda (left fork) or (right fork), a much longer distance, to Tristomo, a now-deserted place after the last two old residents died.

The other track, initially following the road from near where the coaches stop for the photo opportunity of Olymbos, picks up, at the top, the path that cuts down through the multiple bends in the road to emerge on the edge of Diafani. This path is attractive, often through trees and rock faces that have more colour than higher up.

DIAFANI

As my return to Crete involved catching the ferry there, this was the route I took down to Diafani and discovered it was invariably in SUN! Half a day and a night there and I was hooked. The Anoixi taverna, in a vine-shaded courtyard behind the front, dishes to be examined in the pots and glorious red wine, with complimentary loukoumades afterwards, certainly helped. Some years later there I met Roger Jinkinson, author of 'Tales from a Greek Island' and its follow-up, a Diafani resident for half the year, the other half spent in deepest mid-Wales. When people ask him if it isn't a bit much living in such an out-of-the-way place as Diafani, he laughs and says at least there he doesn't have to travel half an hour to find a shop. (Not that the shops in Diafani – a couple of dimly-lit mini-markets – are much to write home about, though at least they were open, unlike the one in Olymbos. A fruit and veg van used to come up on the ferry a couple of times a week to serve both places; it may travel by road now).

On my brief initial and accidental visit I also discovered short walks in each direction along the coast, beside the deep greens of the pines and sparkling ones of the olive trees, against the wonderful blue of the sea. This was only the start. A note in my record book says 'extraordinarily pleasant' about this sojourn. Nerveless!

Apart from this, next morning I realised that from rooms up the hill you could watch for the approach of the ferry from Rhodes way out to sea, with sufficient time to walk down and round the harbour. (Big bonus for the nervous – will I miss the boat? – traveller. Unfortunately, it doesn't work quite as well if you're going back to Rhodes as the northbound ferry coming up the coast is hidden until fairly close) There were, however, a couple of nerve-awakening bits on this visit (in fact that's something else Diafani has a store of – sorry). First the computer went down so that getting a ticket looked in doubt, though it came back to life in time (Computerised ticketing became compulsory some decades ago after a couple of ferries were found to have more than a thousand passengers above their allowance. The downside to all this is that paying on board is banned and it's wise to buy a ticket the day before sailing, if you can. On one of my early trips to Diafani there were no tickets left on the morning of departure – although some appeared at the last minute – but in those days there were two ferries on the same day so there was no disaster).

The second issue, on the way, was that, with the wind at Bofor 7-8 and spray coming over the top deck – and the 'Ierapetra' was a big ship – it didn't stop at the next small island, Kassos. With the later ferry a few days away, this *was* one for the nerves. It obviously didn't affect me then but did play on my mind (naturally) when I planned to go to Kassos a couple of years later. Since I'd had experience of this sort of problem some years earlier on Amorgos (to follow) it wasn't just a baseless fear.

So next year I was back and, with more of this serendipity that Diafani keeps giving – the place I'd stayed in the previous year was full – stumbled on Nikos' Hotel at the top of the hill. Great location with fabulous views over the village and sea. Nikos also runs the village travel agency and boat trips to the nearby beaches but especially to the now-deserted island of Saria to the north (more below). An important man in the village, Nikos is a fierce guardian of the area's traditional heritage and paths, and a mine of knowledge. He remembers as a youngster a hairy boat trip (and almost a shipwreck) to the north which included Kevin Andrews, author of 'The Flight of Ikaros', the devastating account of his travels in the Mani during the Civil War, who lived in Diafani for some years. (Roger Jinkinson has written an excellent biography of Kevin, who was later to drown swimming off Kapsali in Kythera).

One of Nikos' proudest possessions (in keeping for the village) is a copy of a tablet held in the British Museum (boos allowed here) which was found at Vrougounda and inscribed by a doctor (Samos?) in antiquity.

This second year I decided the 20-hour door-to-door-in-one-go and arrive-in-the-middle-of-the-night experience was one to forgo so stayed the night in Sitia and caught a ferry mid-morning – and on time! – to arrive in late afternoon at Diafani.

One of the delights of Diafani-Olymbos is that not only have many of the local footpaths been preserved, they are also sign-posted (invaluable for the nervous/gormless walker, prone to getting lost: no guesses allowed). The first morning I set off up the path to Olymbos as far as the road over to Avlona (in about an hour), then took a path, opposite the abandoned quarry, that runs parallel to the road down. From there I went on down to Vrougounda, with some rock-cut tombs – and a chapel that each year at the end of August hosts a festival. Many people, especially from Diafani, go by boat, quite a few sleeping out there for the night.

It was less than three hours to Vrougounda, the way back up being a bit of a slog and delayed slightly by wild donkeys blocking the path (Nervous moment but it passed). By following red dots through the village, I came out on one of the paths, through the pine forest, down to Vananda beach, a short walk along the coast to Diafani. One stretch of these paths from Avlona still retains the old kalderimi, in excellent condition and its sizeable blocks of cut stone a joy to follow.

Then followed my first trip to Saria. In some ways the most eventful. There was wind (of course) so the sea was a touch rough (I'm not trying to put you off). Keeping close to the shore meant there was a good deal of shelter, but it was too rough for the small boat to enter the sea cave on the way. (Bit of relief for the nerves, that)

Saria has probably been deserted now for thirty years or more but once had a thriving hamlet, Argos, in the north. It is separated from Karpathos by a narrow (150m?) channel, Steno, through which a strong current flows. In the past, as pictured on the panels of the fountain in Diafani near the Gorgona taverna (see back cover), cattle were swum across to Saria to pasture.

Unless the boat diverts to Agia Ekaterini on the northern tip of Karpathos to drop off walkers going back to Diafani (see later) or to Agios Spiridon in a bay at the southern end of Saria for walkers intending to cross the island (also later), it proceeds up the east coast of Saria to the bay of Palatia, the anchorage for Argos, where there's a barbecue lunch and opportunity for swimming.

The first time we put into Palatia a beautiful young girl appeared – was this Calypso's island? So much for uninhabited. It wasn't the nerves that were set jangling. Then her (also Italian) boyfriend arrived: they spent the night there as a jaunt from Diafani.

On the hillside above the bay are strange beehive-shaped buildings, whose origin and age no one knows. Arab pirates? The valley ends in a gorge leading up to Argos, where a number of the houses are still in fairly good condition. From there a path leads out to the edge of the cliff, with a small chapel overlooking the bay.

The barbecue (bifteki, in this case, rissoles, and salad) usually features uninvited guests (don't panic, not mossies): wild goats and sometimes wild donkeys (their time came later on this occasion). Anything left lying about was prey for the goats and constant vigilance was needed. One that strayed too close was grabbed by Nikos, who gave a demonstration on how to milk one. We were content to watch. Later, as another of his skills, Nikos caught an octopus, for cooking that evening at his brother's taverna on the front in Diafani.

When we prepared to leave, wild donkeys came down to forage and as people were getting back on the boat, the dog which, some woman had brought along, managed to find itself among the donkeys and received a kick from a flailing hoof. Cue blood and wailing. I'm not sure if it was Nikos who saved the dog – probably – but the drama on the voyage wasn't over there.

By late afternoon the sun has dipped behind Saria and as the wind had risen it was cold with lots of spray. A cheap poncho helped but didn't survive the trip. Nor did the boat, almost. The link to the rudder broke, meaning that it was impossible to steer from the wheel. No matter (just as you were starting to worry), Nikos solved the problem by standing on the rudder board he exposed at the stern and steering that way. We were a bit late getting back but in time to savour the octopus which he cooked for a few of us. An intriguing day and reassuring to know that when you're in the hands of a master, nervousness takes a back seat.

The following day I set out to walk up to Tristomo, at that time still occupied by the last old couple. The route, initially up the hill and round the school, was the one I'd followed on my first afternoon in Diafani the year before. Winding among trees, on and off the dirt road to Vananda and invariably with that deep blue sea on your right, it's a truly delightful half-hour walk. Vananda has a scattering of houses and a small kafenion in the trees behind the beach (though it was his 'Later' when asked if there was any food on that same first afternoon – at 1.45! – that drove me back to discover the Anoixi: more serendipity)

Beyond Vananda, at a place known as Xiloskala – no idea why since, unlike at the Samaria Gorge, there wasn't even any sign of wooden handrails – the path had for many years ceased to exist after the slopes below were dynamited in the late 80s for stone for the ferry dock (Prior to that, as Roger Jinkinson recounts of his first visit to Diafani, you were decamped into a small boat in the bay – which is how he met Nikos). However, the local community had rebuilt the path across the broken area so that the traditional link to the north was restored. Done presumably for visitors as the need for locals was long past. Filoxenia – true hospitality.

I never made it to Tristomo – and still haven't, after several attempts by different routes. A wide track ascends from Vananda and meanders along the side of the hill, past fields and olive groves before becoming an undulating path through the trees. Then I came to what might have been Xiloskala (though the Rough Guide suggests it's further north and consists of stone-built stairs, which must be unlikely as they show no sign of disturbance – that was only mine). The path was across scree and probably passable, though with a slope down a few hundred metres to the sea and bearing in mind that I'd have to return this way, discretion (call that fear, who needs nerves?) became the better part of valour (who am I kidding?) and I turned back.

I was to traverse this route the following year but Xiloskala was the least of the nervous stresses. In fact I'm not even sure I noticed it as I was hurrying back to see the Austrian girls, Brigitta and Waltrat, whom I'd met the previous year on the Saria 'octopus' trip and seen on several occasions in the Anoixi, before they caught their ferry back to Pigardia and home – via direct flight to Graz!

I'd requested Nikos, on his way with a party to Saria, to drop me at Agia Ekaterini so that I could do the walk back to Diafani. No problem, until he asked me as we neared the shore whether I wanted dropping at the 'Point' or on the beach. How was I to know? If I wanted the Point, I'd have to jump off the boat. That made deciding easier. But if I got off on the beach, was there a path to the quay. 'Of course', said Nikos. 'Go along the beach.' And I believed him. (See Book 2, The Gullible Traveller)

The beach, that is a slightly less rocky bit of a mass of boulders, was gained via a small ladder let down at an awkward angle from the prow. Into the water. I was halfway down and regretting not choosing the jump option when one of the group, a walker, said 'Take your boots off. They won't dry.' Halfway down a ladder? 'And throw them on the beach,' he added. I managed the boots, but one sock landed in the water. Then I was down, in shallow water and retrieving the wet sock. Fortunately, I had a spare inner in my rucksac. Relief at last. Or was it?

The mass of boulders around me had fallen over time from the sizeable cliffs behind me. Could I change my mind? I looked round. The boat was disappearing rapidly. Robinson Crusoe came to mind. It wasn't even a Friday. I dried my feet and put on my boots. 'Just go along the beach', Nikos had said. Some hope, the boulders spilled into the sea. The was a sort of path a few metres in from the shore so I followed that. Thanks Nikos. The path ended, in a ten-foot gap with deep water below. Retreat. I scrambled up the rocks and ploughed on over boulders. At times a faint path appeared. Then disappeared. By trial and error, after half an hour I reached the Point, which was a small jetty. Probably quite easy to jump down onto.

I don't recall feeling nervous. Triumph of will over matter? It was more like terror. If I *was* trapped, the boat would probably pass by in six hours. And, if I remembered correctly from the previous year, some way out at sea from here. Still, I was on solid ground. There was a memorial slab at the rear of the jetty. I don't think my Greek was good enough to make any sense of it. Fortunately, I expect, as it was probably to those trapped here in the past who'd starved to death.

Anyway, I was at last ready to proceed. Then I noticed the extremely thin path that zigzagged up the hill. Wide enough for a goat, perhaps, but for me? And over what looked like scree. It made Nikos' beach path resemble a motorway. Despair swept back. Again, I paused for thought. Or, rather, my brain froze.

For some reason I must have glanced behind the memorial. A flight of steps! The relief was overwhelming. I surged up them, not even pausing to look in the small church at the top. Escape was the only thing on my mind. The vague thoughts I'd had of visiting Tristomo before heading south were ditched. And the path from here was good, mainly ascending but well away from any cliffs. Relief.

After an hour I met, coming up, my next-door neighbours from Nikos' Hotel, Dave and Anne, who were intending a round trip via Tristomo. They'd set off at 9.30 (it was now 1pm). I gave them my map as they weren't that sure where they were going and we parted. I wondered if we'd see each other again. (The worry increased when they weren't back by dark: they didn't return until 8.30)

Anyway I was motoring. I thought. Then I came to a steep drop. A hundred feet? More? The despair returned.

There were steps down. Not that wide. And no handrail. I sat down. Not in defeat, to edge down on my bottom. Deep breaths. Involuntary ones. After the first, right-angle turn to get onto the steps, it wasn't bad going. Finally I was down. From that point on the way was straightforward, undulating but without any major panic-inducing sections. As I said earlier, I didn't even notice the loose scree at what might have been the Xyloskala. The only regret I have is that after losing half an hour at the start and hurrying to see the girls before they left, I didn't really take in some of the scenery on the way. I also got through three and three-quarter litres of water on the journey, in three hours from the memorial.

But I made it a few minutes before the boat was due, for a large cold beer and yoghurt and honey. The back of my thighs seized up later but, apart from that, I'd 'survived'. Obviously, merely the nervous traveller's version of an adventure but still etched – make that seared – on the mind. With no desire for a repeat.

The next day (was I mad at that time? It didn't wipe out nervousness, merely shoved it into the background. There must be other cures) I made another attempt at Tristomo via Avlona. The countryside beyond Avlona is remote and uninhabited, though with some evidence of cultivation and there are sheep (one small flock of which I managed to scurry on up the hillside while trying to re-direct them to their shepherd behind). An hour and forty minutes from Avlona I think I was able to look down on Tristomo but gave up at that point – the round-trip was more than six hours.

There are fewer walks to the south of Diafani. The best is to the beach at Papa Minas, about an hour away with plenty of interesting up-and-down sections and some dramatic views to the sea. It starts from the road to the harbour, through the boatyard/tip and winding up and over the headland. Part is on the dirt road although the path takes short cuts across the ravines that the road has to by-pass. Return really has to be the same way: with the benefit of views of the mountains to the north. The map does show an inland route, picking up a track from Diafani.

This track is an alternative route to Olymbos, passing close by the chapel of Agios Konstantinos on a hill before coming out on the main road to the south of Olymbos. However, this route from Diafani lacks shade and, being in a wide valley, hasn't the variation of the main path.

Another route to Olymbos is from the beach at Forokli, further south than Papa Minas but to start you need Nikos to drop you there on the boat. And yes, it **is** a beach. I can't even remember needing to remove my boots to disembark. The walk is not one of the best, being a steepish climb uphill with little, if any, shade.

Besides the section of the path up from Diafani through the woods towards Olymbos, the most rewarding walk is that from Vananda up towards Avlona and then back down via the alternative route that starts at the top, along the track to Avlona. This path follows the dried-up stream bed from Vananda, winding up and down and then climbing through the pines which, on the right day, exude their warm breath. The return includes the kalderimi mentioned above, with glorious views across the pine-clad ridges and hills, and also out to sea. It's a three-to-four-hour trip and, with sun and not too much wind, – you'll be lucky, some of the pines on the ridges are bent almost double from the prevailing winds – is truly exhilarating.

SARIA

Then there's the walk across Saria. Only attempted on my fourth visit there. 2013. Not sure if it was available before or if anyone was being dropped off on previous trips to Saria. Or was I too timid to ask? There were directions in the Rough Guide, so I knew about the possibility but alone on an uninhabited island, come on? The northern tip of Karpathos was bad enough. (And on subsequent trips to Saria I'm sure those cliffs above where I was dropped look bigger every time.)

However, again the Diafani serendipity came into play. I'd planned to go to Saria the day after I arrived but managed to miss the boat! Thought it was a 10.30 departure and it was ten. No problem as Nikos goes there twice a week. And the following Monday a group was going to do the walk. Seven people. Led by Gervaise. The expert, who'd done it several times. What more could nervous walker need?

We were duly dropped off at 11 by Nikos at Agios Spiridon in the bay on the south coast of Saria. No jumping down onto beach or 'Point' but stepping onto the jetty. A gap in the bushes in the centre of the beach led to a rocky path up the hill on the left side of the valley. Further on at the top was the first water stop in an olive grove. From there red dots across the way marked the path that eventually led, past some buildings that looked fairly recent, or at least in good condition, to a small chapel, Agios Andreas, which was the rest stop. We were on the eastern side of the island, with the more mountainous section to our left. It was then down and up and across level ground for some distance, with plenty of evidence of once-cultivated fields either side. Next there was an obligatory diversion for Gervaise to point out the rock arch above the sea below. As it's since collapsed, those who moaned about the delay ('It was his thing,' they muttered), deserved the rebukes from Gervaise.

The sea was now constantly in view as we descended and then passed through an area of pines (the path almost blocked by a fallen tree on my last visit) before climbing, past a vast cave in the cliff and up a steep staircase leading out onto the crest of the hill. From here a path leads straight ahead and then sharply down into Palatia Bay. It's the shortest route but steep, rough and slippery in places. I've done it once (nervous times) but Gervaise insisted on going to the left and following the safer, if longer, route that does eventually give you a view over Argos before taking you down the gorge – interesting in itself – to the beach. In all it's about a three-and-a-half-hour walk, not wildly dramatic but with plenty of variation and a good sense of achievement at the end. Plus the lunch, of course which Nikos remembers to save, if the others have already dined.

I've repeated the walk three times since, once with a larger party which immediately split up so I walked with one other person, who wouldn't have known the way otherwise; once with a German couple and once largely on my own. I say on my own as the other person who got off, Mark, a young, fit-looking Austrian, decided first to go and explore the path at the far side of the bay. It was, however, reassuring to know that he was behind me so, in the event of a problem, he would find me. In fact, that's a good tip for the nervous traveller: always try to have someone behind to pick up the pieces – and, of course, to ease the nerves. If he'd walked with me, he'd no doubt have been faster, so would have left me behind anyway. He had almost caught me up by the top of the steps and then went down the short cut.

After five trips from Crete, in 2013 I switched to Rhodes, there being a ferry, the 'Prevelis', that left Rhodes on a Thursday morning at 8am – which followed conveniently from flights from Birmingham the previous day – and returned the next Tuesday to coincide with the return flight the following Wednesday. These ferry times meant midday arrivals and departures from Diafani (or in one case, arrival at Pigardia –'Karpathos' on ferry schedules – since the 'Prevelis' didn't put in to Diafani, the wind being too strong. While I was reconciled to spending a night in Pigardia and then catching the tourist boat up the next morning – which would have been a forlorn hope as the winds meant they didn't sail for the next three days – I happened on Nikos, who had brought some French guests down to catch the ferry to Piraeus for their return home; and had a scenic ride up the new road to compensate).

For Diafani, the journey time to/from Rhodes is about five hours, less therefore than from Crete but as the routes have changed Crete is often missed out anyway these days. A bonus at Rhodes is not only staying the night at Niki's Pension in the Old Town but being able to eat at the Pizzanos/ Sea Star taverna nearby, with its excellent fava and calamares. Michalis at Niki's is also very welcoming.

There were, however, two nervous-anxiety inducing aspects to sailing from Rhodes, both now happily resolved. The first was that, as Rhodes effectively has three harbours, knowing which one applied (Akandia). The second was buying a ticket. Until the flight times were pushed later in the day, this was no problem as the agents were still open or when the ferry departure was 8.30 there was time to get to an early-opening office at 8 and buy one there. Then it was brought forward to 8. The big question was: are tickets on sale at the port? I'd never noticed any such facility and after my close shave on Sikinos a few years earlier (see later), I was wary – well, a nervous wreck – of trusting to luck and having to dash back up to the main road in search of one. For some reason I discovered that there was, indeed, a ticket office at the port. The only nightmare then was the queue, moving agonisingly slowly as the clock ticked towards eight. I was even accused by some Greek bloke of pushing in. All I was doing was trying to close up since he was dawdling – and, I suspected, had pushed in himself. As ever, the worry was misplaced: the boat didn't leave till half past.

In fact, if you think about it, both worries were groundless. Is there a lesson there? Probably, but can a nervous traveller change its spots?

Karpathos, and specifically Diafani, is one of my favourite places. Even without the same towering mountains of Crete, it has a majesty and beauty of its own and the work of the local community to maintain the best of their traditions means that the welcome is always warm and the stay rewarding.

On the way from Crete I'd been intrigued by the smaller, near-neighbour of Karpathos, Kassos. Partly because I was always trying to visit new islands, partly from its grim history during the War of Independence and partly because of a book about the island, 'The Feasts of Memory' by Elias Kulukundis. So, in 2010, five years after I'd first passed it on my way to and from Karpathos, I set out to stop off there on my way back to Crete.

DODECANESE ISLANDS

KASSOS

You might recall (somewhere above) my first experience of passing Kassos when the wind was high. The ferry didn't stop there. A subsequent, less concerning, experience was arriving back at Sitia at 3am, when the only accommodation open (because it was outside) was a chair at the bus station, waiting for the first bus at 6am. Would my nerves stand the strain of such uncertainty? Clearly not.

This was, however, where nervousness came to be of use. (It may, of course, have been unnecessary but I never needed to find out. That was the point.)

Because, fearful of being stranded for several days (it is a very small island) as the ferry sailed past, I booked my onward travel by air. Fry (pronounced 'Three'), the capital of Kassos, has an airport within walking distance. Worries brushed aside. I could cope with flying. (Otherwise known as ignorance is the Nervy's best friend)

Kassos, the southernmost of the Dodecanese islands, has a somewhat decrepit air, as if it's never really recovered from the devastation of 1824 when, in reprisal for the island's fleet's involvement in the uprising against the Turks three years earlier, the entire population was either massacred or taken to slavery in Egypt. Facing the incongruously large quay at Fry is a fancy-looking two-storey apartment block/hotel. I turned down the offer of a room and turned left along the road to the Flisvos Rooms. A good choice. First nerve test – any rooms on Kassos? – overcome.

There is an old harbour, Emborio, further on but without much sign of life. I followed the road in the opposite direction, towards the airport – safer to check it was still there (You can't be too careful). Then carried on to a small beach, with a couple of sad-looking umbrellas and red clay visible below the thin layer of sand.

A road led from there uphill to one of the handful of villages on the island, Agia Marina, again without much sign of life and where I managed to get lost, thinking I was east of Fry when I was still west. I retraced my way back via the airport. The countryside to the south-west, and in fact all the way round to the north of the island, consists of barren hills-cum-mountains of 1000 to 2000 feet. It wasn't inviting roaming country, though the people were pleasant and welcoming – they probably don't see enough tourists to be sick of them.

Fry has an interesting small museum in a Kassiot house and an excellent taverna, Mylos, overlooking the port.

However, the principal feature of my short stay on Kassos was the departure. Despite having tested the length of the walk (20 minutes?), I was first there, sometime before the plane was due, or the only other passenger, a woman with a baby, arrived.

Although there was an attractive brick building beside the runway that looked as if it might be a new terminal, the existing one in 2010 (and with the crisis still to come) was a one-storey shack. Adjoining it was perhaps the airport's unique characteristic, at least in western Europe – an outside toilet. (Yes, course I tried it – very serviceable – you never know how long you might have to wait for the next.)

Inside, the one room was divided in two by a security screen and a short conveyer belt. As you walked in, a huge set of scales stood beside the desk. Check-in was, as you might expect, quick, then you could go outside and look around: the red plastic chairs in the 'departure lounge' didn't look that enticing.

As Karpathos was clearly visible to the north west, it was possible to watch the plane as it took off from there and approached – not that high above the sea, I have to say. Was there a twinge of tension? My brain had probably seized up again.

Passing through security and walking down to board was also reassuringly smooth: small airports do have that advantage. Once on board there were a couple of surprises: the standard security procedure and a full cabin service – well, a drink and a packet of biscuits. The pilot announced that we'd be in the air for nine minutes – it was billed as a forty-minute flight – and we were hardly airborne before the stewardess was passing down, dispensing orange juice and the said biscuits. I only realised why the locals weren't opening theirs when she returned moments later – it was probably a 24-seater plane and half-full – to collect the rubbish: there was barely time to get the packet open let alone eat the biscuits.

But a nerveless experience and one to linger in the memory.

As Kassos is the southernmost of the Dodecanese islands it's northwards past Karpathos to see the rest. Although Rhodes is the next one north, the ferry calls at Halki first, to the west of its larger neighbour, before its destination at Akandia harbour.

HALKI

Less than half the size of Kassos and barely thirty square kilometres in extent, Halki, otherwise known (to me) as Islington-on-Sea, is little more than the port town of the same name and owes its continuing existence almost entirely to tourism – a UK company, now defunct, having focused on it from the 1980s. It has a brighter air than Kassos because most of the houses have been renovated to meet this new market. Full of middle-class Brits playing at being on a Greek island, it therefore doesn't reek of Greekness and is prone to wind if your accommodation happens to be exposed.

That said, if all you want is a villa with a ladder down into the sea, a newly-created sandy beach a short walk away and plenty of tavernas then, although there are alternatives elsewhere, you'll be happy enough. Only the wind might make you stressed. Your nerves shouldn't be too troubled.

Most of the population decamped to Tarpon Springs in Florida years ago, a detail indicated by the name of the only road into the interior. This, besides leading to a monastery (overnight stays possible for the 'monastery experience') at the northern tip of the island, passes the remains of a castle, stuck prominently on the edge of a towering cliff about half an hour's walk from the town, with dizzying views down and, if the weather is clear, towards Karpathos.

(The mention of Tarpon Springs does remind us that emigration was traditionally the only salvation for many Greeks over the past hundred years. Different islands had their own destinations – in Diafani it was Baltimore, US; for many it was Australia, so that Melbourne has claims to be the third-biggest Greek city in the world. Often the father would go, to work, sending back money and perhaps returning once a year, if that. A fascinating book, probably now out-of-print, entitled 'A Place for Us', by Nicholas Gage, author of 'Eleni', the search for the killers of his mother during the Civil war, graphically depicts the emigrant life in the US and the fight to succeed.)

The only other excursion on Halki used to be a boat trip to a neighbouring uninhabited island for its sandy beach and a barbecue. Hardly Saria.

While the main ferry twice a week heads up the west coast of Rhodes to Rhodes town, an hour and a half away, the link to Halki for package trips was from Kamiros Skala, a small port-village almost opposite and an interesting short journey.

There's apparently not much short-stay accommodation on Halki, although there may be now the package business has reduced. A week felt like a long time.

So it's on to Rhodes.

RHODES

Rodos, in Greek, is the largest of the Dodecanese islands, was one of the earliest Greek islands to be developed for mass tourism and still has considerable on-going development. That means a lot of ugly, gigantic hotels, especially along the beach strip between the airport and Rhodes town but also, increasingly to the south of the town, to Lindos and beyond. With its history attracting huge cruise ships, getting a feel for the 'real' Rodos can be difficult.

However, the back streets of the Old Town retain their charm and Greek life continues largely undisturbed, if you can find it. Fortunately, my friends Martin and Ruth, Martin a former colleague in the early 80s, have a house in Koskinou on the edge of Rhodes Town and visits to them have opened up access to local Greek life. Their wonderful neighbours, Haris and Natalie, exemplify the struggle Greeks have been going through since the crisis started to bite in 2011, with jobs hard to come by and taxes spiralling as the EU demanded its pound(s) of flesh (bone and blood).

An unexpected aspect of this came in a tourist taverna of one of their friends in the Old Town. The menu wasn't overly attractive, in fact we were reduced to pizza after the starters but when the bill came, I thought Martin had miscalculated: it said 92€ but he was only gathering 68. When I asked, he said 'Oh, no, that's the tourist price. We pay the local rate'. One way the Greeks can survive.

Some places, seen from a local's view, have a different and more positive dimension from their often dubious reputation. For instance, Faliraki. Like Malia in Crete and Kavos in Corfu, Faliraki is principally known for the excesses of its mainly young visitors, who are not there usually for the culture. (On a flight to Rhodes years ago, when the pilot announced that we'd shortly be landing in Rhodes, a girl shrieked 'But I'm not going to Rhodes, I'm going to

Faliraki!') However, on a visit there with Martin and Ruth, albeit in daytime and to an Australian-run bar of friends, it was a surprisingly relaxed and friendly place. Nightime nervous breakdowns only.

Local tavernas in and around Koskinou provide much more authentic eating experiences, both in their offerings and their atmosphere.

History there is aplenty, both in Rhodes Town and around the island. The city walls are still remarkably intact and impressive, while within them a couple of mosques have been renovated and the evidence of the Knights of St John, who ruled the island for nearly two centuries, is striking. The architectural museum is both atmospheric, being housed in a former hospital of the Knights, and with some fine exhibits. Outside the walls and about a half hour's walk away are the remains of the ancient city, with a stadium and surviving temple arch, possibly owing a lot to Mussolini's cultural ambitions. Ialyssos is another ancient site to explore.

To the south, at Lindos, the Acropolis is striking if a bit tarted up and busy in recent years. In the past, especially on a Sunday, the (no longer) free day, it could be a serene place in which to sit and gaze at the sea.

As indicated earlier, Rhodes' main nerves-shaking elements were its three (or four) harbours and which to choose. Once clarified, onward destinations await.

SYMI

Symi, a delightful little island about the same size as Kassos but with a lot more to savour, is just about the nearest, and most accessible from Rhodes, although it's almost surrounded by fingers of the Turkish mainland. (Don't panic, they're not at war any more) In fact, Symi has to be accessed from Rhodes, having no airport of its own, probably from being too rocky to host one. It is also a day-trip destination from Rhodes though the crowds rarely seem obtrusive.

Symi's first, stunning, feature is the harbour at Symi Town/Yialos, with grand, colourful mansions ranged on the hillside around the bay. For many years, after Symi fell on hard times in the Twentieth Century, a majority of these houses sank into disrepair and, even twenty years ago, a good deal of dereliction could be seen. However, more recent renovations, even if for tourist purposes, have created a vibrant feel to the town. Behind it, the several hundred steps of the Kallistrata lead up to the old town, Horio, from where the road runs down to Pedi, a beach village at the head of a deep narrow bay. These are the main settlements.

You'll probably struggle not to be at ease here, though accommodation without aircon at the height of summer might do it. Otherwise, wandering around Yialos – there is also a beach round the headland and you can walk on along the coast to Emborio – is a stress-free activity. A small bus makes regular runs up to Horio and then down to Pedi, if the climb is too much. The walk down to Pedi from Horio is only about twenty minutes and a fairly gentle climb back.

Both Yialos and Horio have a profusion of good tavernas, most of which haven't yet succumbed to trendiness. In Pedi the main accommodation is the Pedi Beach Hotel, comfortable and fronting the beach. From Pedi you can walk to a couple of small, nearby beaches, Agios Nikolaos along the right-hand bank of the bay or Agia Marina, a bit further, following the left-hand bank and then up and over the hill. An inexpensive boat trip to Agia Marina is probably preferable and the ride is certainly enjoyable. Both have tavernas and Agios Nikolaos some shade under tamarisk trees. Tasteful development at Agia Marina provides sunshades and easy access to the sea, while the taverna is a delight.

Boat trips also serve more remote beaches down the coast, such as Nanou, though there's not much shade until the sun disappears behind the high cliffs – they're rumoured to have been a model for 'The Guns of Navarone' (See later, Leros). Don't panic, the guns aren't likely to topple over onto you.

Much of the rest of the island is bare rock, although re-afforestation has reduced this and it doesn't give a sense of being barren and uninviting. On one occasion a guided walk, starting from Horio, crossed the island through shaded and cultivated countryside to an unfrequented bay, where a boat waited for the return.

There are enough sights, whether of buildings or land and sea, easily to occupy a week; a day trip would probably be a rush and not fully appreciate the island's charms.

TILOS

Though not much further from Rhodes than Symi, Tilos, out in the open sea, feels more remote. Fertile and traditionally an agricultural island, its tourism development has been more recent and more low-rise and low-key. Tilos is unlikely to over-stress you, nor over-excite you particularly. (Mind you, it is the only place where I've seen a cockroach, so you might want to test yourself there).

At the beginning of this century the island had its own boat, 'The Sea Star', to bring people from Rhodes. It's now served, usually twice a week, by the fast catamaran 'Dodekanissos Express' on its way up to Kos (from Kolona Harbour in Rhodes). Your nerves might object to the way it can roll but views from the open top deck may also be exhilarating.

The port and main town, Livadia, extends now round a deep bay backed by low hills. Coffee beside the beach is a principal activity. An island coach tour will take you to the 'capital', Megalo Horio, little more than a small village, and then on to a monastery at the end of the road. It will also call at the cave where evidence of dwarf elephants was found in the 70s; the museum in Megalo Horio has some remains.

It's possible to walk round the coast in both directions. Going north, a path leads to Lethra, where it turns inland up a dried-up river valley before joining the road back to Livadia. Following the road round the other side of the bay takes you up into the hills: the highest peak is less than two thousand feet; return is the same way after reaching an abandoned village in a couple of hours, if you carry on that far. It's not an especially scenic or dramatic route. Equally, climbing to the south, you'll come to the ridge beside one of several ruined castles and have a view of the sea.

Livadia has several good tavernas to aid your stress-free stay.

NISSIROS

The next island going north, Nissiros is a not-quite extinct volcano (OK, calm down, the last major eruption was in 1878 but if you've been missing feeling stressed on Tilos, this will give you something to worry about). Another feature that might give you palpitations is the profusion of signs in Russian: you're unlikely to be kidnapped by the KGB, however, but it did make me wonder whether learning Greek was the right move.

Having said this, Nissiros is actually an enjoyable island to visit and many people do on day trips from Kos – to see the volcano. A line of coaches waits on the quay for the tourist boats to arrive, then there usually follows some chaos as they sort out their various loads before setting off up into the hills.

The volcano experience can be disconcerting and disappointing (no, not because there's no lava flow). Since you're already on the volcano (it's the island), when you crest the hill what you see is not some Vesuvius-like shape but a wide valley-bowl with an extensive flat base, in the middle of which, bare and of baked yellow mud, are some smaller craters with wisps of sulphurous gas emerging.

The coach drops you beside the biggest of these, Stephanos, and you can walk down into the crater – it's only about twenty-five metres deep – and approach the holes (not too closely, obviously, you don't want to risk falling in or being overcome by the sulphurous gases, do you?) from which some bubbling sounds – and smells – issue. Not your characteristic image of a volcano, to be sure.

The visit is usually only about half an hour and in your disorientation – or is it the fumes? – you may not think to look at the other nearby, smaller, crater, Porfiros.

The rest of Nissiros is certainly not disappointing. The main town, and port, Mandraki, perches on the island's north-west corner. The excellent Three Brothers Rooms, facing onto the harbour, provides glorious views out to sea and, over to the left, a glimpse of the intriguing small island of Yialos, a white shape as it's being quarried for its pumice stone. Weekend boats provide day trips.

At the far end of the main street, which narrows as it weaves through the older part of town, a Venetian castle and monastery cling to the cliff face but the real surprise is a twenty-minute walk uphill: the ancient kastro, with stunning Cyclopian walls and an arched gateway. There's not much remaining inside but the grandeur of the walls is astonishing in itself.

When the day-trippers have gone, Nissiros has a pleasant, relaxed feel, with some agreeable tavernas that are hardly busy at night. The island also has a newish, impressive museum.

Kos

Like Rhodes, one of the earliest and so heavily-developed tourist destinations, Kos, with several large resorts along its south coast, does, nevertheless, have some intriguing historical sites and, as a hub on the ferry network going north and south, often requires an overnight stay in the main centre, Kos Town. The Hotel Karis, down the long street at the back of the harbour (roughly opposite the land-train terminus), is a pleasant, good value hotel for this purpose, away from the more raucous collections along the beach road. And more soothing on the nerves.

The centre of Kos Town is itself an archaeological site, the agora with a jumble of ruins, thanks to periodic earthquakes (none recently, oh, hang on, er… not since 2017) knocking things over. The shell of a Venetian castle stands next to the harbour while nearby is the so-called Hippocrates' plane tree, beneath which the father of medicine supposedly practised two and a half thousand years ago. Thought to be about 700 years old, the chances of that having happened are therefore nil but, with its branches supported by rusting metal scaffolding, it radiates welcome shade and atmosphere. Also nearby is a former Turkish bath house in better repair.

Kos's position, with mountainous arms of the Turkish mainland to either side, has a certain dramatic feel. On the edge of the town are the Western excavations and across the road a rebuilt Roman Odeon.

About four kilometres out of town is the Asklepion, site of the ancient centre of healing and dedicated to the God of healing, Asklepios. Now invariably crowded, its main attribute is its location, with views across from the highest terrace to the Turkish mainland, in those days, of course, Greek Anatolia. Since Bodrum opposite became so built-up, the perspective is not quite as spiritual.

Kos Town can be lively without feeling overwhelming and it's always possible to find peace away from the crowds if you need to. It's only a short ferry hop to the next island to the north

KALIMNOS

Less brash than its bigger neighbour to the south, Kalimnos is a medium-sized island with a history as leading centre for sponge-fishing. Pothia, the capital and port, is clustered round a wide bay at the south of the island, with a ring of hills behind. A bustling, lively, working port, its narrow streets, despite a one-way system, give it a rather hectic air (Warning for the nervous: don't step off the pavement without looking). While

Loutro, South Crete

Symi, Yialos

Leros, Kastro

Moni Hozoviotissa, Amorgos

the centre of the seafront is dominated by a couple of large, undistinguished hotels, Pothia does have some accommodation of character. The Greek House, somewhere up to the left, had a room set on the roof (access via a narrow, outdoor set of stairs, safe enough – really – but a bit of a squeeze). Without air-conditioning – and the landlady reckoned it had been 43 degrees during the day – the room's window layout to allow a flow of air meant it was perfectly cool.

A larger possibility is the Villa Melina, a house of character inland to the right and with studio rooms in the garden. This is not far from the very impressive archaeological museum, if you can find it open, which has a collection of stunning statuary.

Pothia also has a couple of good tavernas, if they're still there: Ksefteris, hidden away down an alley to the right of the harbour (looking inland) and, more centrally, Pandellis; both outdoor venues.

The bus up the west coast goes to a pair of adjacent, small, low-key resorts, including Mirities, from where a short taxi-boat hop takes you to

TELENDOS

Once joined to Kalimnos until an earthquake separated them, Telendos is little more than a five square-kilometre chunk of rock sticking up out of the sea. However, a number of tavernas front the channel and it's possible to walk through the village street to the opposite coast, where there's a beach, Hohklaka. Walking along the coast facing Kalimnos is relaxing, though it's really an hour and a half stroll, returning the same way.

But, another inhabited island (pop 90?) and it's unlikely to stress you. Even if you miss a taxi-boat, there'll be another in half an hour. A pleasant way to spend a couple of hours.

The next island north, and barely separated from Kalimnos, has more surprises.

LEROS

Leros has always had a bad press, both within Greece and internationally but it is something of a gem. The reputation derives from its use to house mental patients and in particular the scandal in the late eighties when a television documentary team exposed the appalling conditions in which the patients were being held. A clean-up followed but the mud stuck and rumour has it that underfunding since the crisis means that conditions there are not currently ideal. One consequence of the scandal appears to be that the patients are now more well-hidden.

Refugees from Syria seem to be taking their place, though, if anyone had the wit and the will, the refugees' presence provides an opportunity. This is because depopulation is evident even in the urban sectors of Leros: Platanos, the sort-of-capital on a ridge in the centre of the island, had more empty shops than Wolverhampton in 2013. Re-housing refugees and using their skills could re-invigorate the place. A village in Italy has undertaken such a scheme but the intricacies of Greek property ownership probably make replication here unlikely.

A more common source of anxiety on Leros is that it has two ports and, despite the fact that, in theory, large ferries use Lakki while smaller ones and hydrofoils use Agia

Marina, it's never quite that simple. Never fear, hoteliers, who will generally take you to the port, tend to know what's happening where.

Leros has plenty of history, though, perhaps unusually for a Greek island, most of it is more recent than ancient. Platanos, and much of the island, is dominated by the Byzantine Kastro, hugely imposing and offering wonderful views, though it's largely a shell now. What makes the walk up from Platanos doubly pleasing is the museum of iconography beside it. While the subject may not sound like the most exciting you'll want to come across, it is enlivened by the guided tour from a Leros-born Texan who uses his tablet to good effect, illustrating obscure details on some of the icons – a surprising number of which turn out to show a considerably-dark-skinned Jesus.

If you're insufficiently disorientated by this, he suddenly produces an image of a twentieth century Commonwealth war grave and asks you to guess its interest (don't spoil his fun now I'm letting you into the secret). The grave in question (in the Allied war cemetery at nearby Krithoni) is that of the father of Ginger Baker, drummer of Cream, killed in the later stages of the 1943 Battle of Leros. (Of which, more to follow).

While much of Leros's charm comes from its indented coastline of small bays, its architecture gives it an unusual distinction. Under Italian rule, in the 1920s and 30s the great natural harbour of Lakki was developed into a naval base, while the town itself was graced with many 'Art Deco' buildings, some of which are now being restored after years of neglect. With a wide, tree-lined avenue leading into the town, Lakki has a grandeur that is undermined to an extent by its absence of much life.

(A non-historical note: the headland at the entrance to the bay is reliably claimed to have given Alistair McLean the inspiration for his novel 'The Guns of Navarone' though, as ever, the fictional version is more dramatic than the original)

Both Lakki and Agia Marina are easily walkable from Platanos, even if the steep downhill road to Agia Marina lacks any pavement towards the bottom.

Although Alinda, Krithoni and Pantelli are the major holiday spots, the Hotel Elefteria in Platanos is an excellent place to stay. Run by a Greek-Danish couple, its roof-top swimming pool is delightful and the food is good. A room with a view of the Kastro is a bonus: especially at night when it's lit up.

The hotel's unique feature is the inclusion, on the ground floor, of a one-room war museum, assembled by the proprietor, Andonis', father, Tassos, who was seven at the time of the Battle and who also remembers the 'Peina', Hunger, that followed. While there are a couple of other, larger war museums on the island, Tassos' collection of letters and books has a personal element that is moving.

(The Battle of Leros, described in the title of its principal history by Anthony Rogers, as 'Churchill's Folly', was a kind of mini-Battle of Crete, in which an under-provisioned and under-prepared British garrison was defeated by a German invasion in November 1943; Churchill's aim having been to secure Kos and Leros before the Germans could exploit the gap left by Italy's recent surrender. Unfortunately, the resources didn't match the idea – shades of Gallipoli – and only a timely surrender avoided greater loss of life).

Because of the island's small size, many of the key points in the Battle can be easily identified. The Hotel Elefteria has a sketch map of the Merovigli area on the hill behind the hotel, where the British headquarters was located in tunnels. A half hour walk brings you to a sign saying 'Military area, no entry'. I was told it was OK to go on and passed one exit of the tunnel (But naturally didn't dare to go in, or linger for long on the top, though again I was told that no one bothered any more.)

A couple of interesting aspects of the Battle are, first, that a German paratroop landing turned the tide after a British signal, sent in 'clear' (ie not in code), indicated they were in trouble. It was always said that, after the Battle of Crete, German paratroops were never used as such again. This was obviously the exception. Secondly, the German forces were commanded by General Muller, original target of the Leigh Fermor kidnap bid, who was to be executed after the war for his murderous actions when Commandant in Crete.

The war museum in Merikia, a short walk from Lakki, is housed in tunnels the Italians originally built to store explosives. Although mainly consisting of equipment and weaponry, there is an interesting video of air attacks on Leros prior to the Battle. The other war museum is located in the Villa Belleni in Alinda, north of Agia Marina, and which has useful maps on display of the Battle's progress. (It also has a room displaying gynaecological instruments, if your nerves need a jolt) On the way there you'll pass the immaculate Allied war cemetery at Krithoni, with 180 or so graves.

Taxis are easy to find – there's a taxi station in Platanos – and cheap. One is needed to visit the little church at Agios Isodoros, beyond Alinda off the road up to the airport. At the end of a short causeway, the church, and the bay, is a pretty spot.

The newish small archaeological museum on the road down to Agia Marina has interesting exhibits attractively displayed about the older history of the island.

The square in Platanos also has an excellent gyros place for lunch, and is a haunt of the tiny British expat community (Leros was a cheap destination). An island to be enjoyed, if you're not worrying (unnecessarily) about the departure port. Then to

LIPSI

A small island to the east of Patmos, Lipsi should be sufficiently laid-back to soothe your nerves, though as there's little to do other than laze about, it may give you too much time to think of something to worry over. A spurious claim to be the island of Calypso aside, there is little of historical interest and walks to the beaches take barely an hour. Apparently, most people come on day trips from Patmos and that probably gives you plenty of time for a taste of it. Two nights and a day were more than enough. One island – like a number of others – mainly for island-bagging. Its larger neighbour to the west has more of interest.

PATMOS

Of similar shape to Leros, with a heavily-indented coastline and lots of small bays, Patmos has a more reverential reputation because of its Biblical associations: it was the island where St John wrote the Book of the Apocalypse. This tends to dominate, not least through the monastery-fortress dedicated to the Saint on the hill above the main port-town, Skala, which sits on a narrow isthmus in the centre of the island. To the west of Skala, and barely a ten-minute walk, you can climb to the ancient kastro, with views as far as Ikaria (and Amorgos?) in the distance or visit the beach at Hohklakas. In these places you can glimpse the true attractiveness of the island.

But the main trip, of course, is to the monastery, or rather, monasteries, since the cave in which St John wrote has had one, the Monastery of the Apocalypse, built round his cave. It's a pleasant, not unduly steep uphill walk (though most cruise ship visitors are bussed there), partly on a path through shaded woods. The cave, which you come to first, has a magical atmosphere (if not full of tourists); somewhat done-up nowadays and lit, it retains an intimate feel. The curious thing about it, as you realise when you emerge and gaze down the hill and out to sea, is how someone looking at that view could be obsessed with the end of the world. Maybe his exile from Ephesus weighed heavily.

Continuing up the hill to Hora and the walls of the Monastery of St John, grimness becomes more of a feature, though inside the place is quite welcoming. It houses a considerable collection of rare manuscripts besides the Treasury and wandering around the parts of the walls (they clearly did their job to deter marauders) you're allowed on, is pleasurable. Once more, the views are spectacular.

Nicholas' new rooms to the north of Skala are very pleasant and the nearby taverna H Netia was excellent. If you're not sent into a tailspin by the reminder of the apocalypse, it's a pleasant island (when cruise ships are absent).

Once reason for re-visiting Patmos was the discovery that on a Friday the small ferry 'Nissos Kalymnos' goes to the nearby island of Arki in the morning and returns later the same afternoon, allowing for an island day-trip.

I'd been intrigued by Arki since, years previously on the 'Nissos Kalymnos' heading south, the ferry hadn't been scheduled to stop at the island. At that time it apparently had no quay for ferries and any visitors, on the rare occasions ferries called, were decamped into small boats. Now there was a quay (the EU again) and the opportunity to see what I'd missed. That turned out not to have been a lot.

ARKI

It's a journey of less than an hour from Patmos. The 'Nissos Kalymnos' is one of that generation of 'real' boats that by now is being pensioned off (EU rules!) and replaced by the big Korean-built giants that don't always give the same authentic sea-going experience (though see Ikaria) ie they have facilities, don't get stuck in port if the weather's bad, or break down.

The new harbour at Arki is in an attractive little bay, out of sight of any habitation. A short walk around the corner, however, brought the port village into sight, with three tavernas beside the beach (one even with rooms). First stop, Nicholas (no relation) taverna, coffee. All very stress-free.

Then it was off to explore. I'd read somewhere that inland were the ruins of a castle in which Julius Caesar had been held after kidnap by pirates (No, really). Upon the payment of a ransom and release, he'd apparently told his captors that he'd return one day and wipe them out. Which he did. (Another, and possibly more authentic version of this story locates it on Farmakonissi, to the east of Lipsi, but that's off the ferry route and perhaps exclusively for military use now, being close to the Turkish mainland. The pirates may not have been big on names anyway.)

Although the lad in the taverna reckoned that the castle was a good three-hour round-trip away, I set off up the main street, past the one (very) mini-market and a couple of houses but it ended in a farmyard at the top of the hill. Naturally I was too nervous to venture inside. (Animals, very risky, humans more so)

Giving up, I took a track off to the left by the mini-market. It ended, fairly soon, past the helipad, at the refuse tip (small). No sign of a track anywhere. Continuing across the scrub I came to a cliff (low, Arki is unusual in being all low-level).

So it was back to Nicholas for a good Greek salad for lunch and more reading.

After lunch I walked south for some way, with a view across to the island of Marathi, destination of beach boats from Patmos but no link to Arki. I even passed a house.

I didn't want to walk too far – fear of missing 'Nissos Kalymnos' and being marooned here for a week – so returned once more to Nicholas for a beer before strolling back in good time (remember, you couldn't see the port from the taverna) to the quay for the boat.

It was late (another of the endearing features of the older boats, how do you think I became nervous?) though not by much. While waiting, however, I spoke to a Greek who'd found the castle: he said it was merely a heap of stones and there was no path to it. An adventure missed? Hmm. Still, a peaceful island, if you want to get away from it all and certainly a relaxing day-trip.

On the earlier occasion when the ferry had passed by Arki and aroused my interest, it had called before that at Agathonisi, another intriguing island, at twice the size (13 sq km) and with twice the population (100) of Arki. However, a guide-book suggested there might not be any rooms, so fear (again, of being stuck: the next ferry would be in three days) prevented my tasting it.

Although these last few islands are the northernmost of the Dodecanese, there is one other in the group (whose actual number still eludes me) and that far to the south from here. This is Kastelorizo, improbably a good hundred kilometres and four hours by ferry east of Rhodes along the south-west coast of Turkey, from which it is separated by only a few kilometres of sea.

KASTELORIZO

The journey is probably worthwhile since the island has a good deal of interest. In the Nineteenth Century it grew in prosperity, thanks to its majestic harbour on the sea route from Europe to the East. Its population reached more than ten thousand. However, following its transfer from Ottoman rule to Italian, a series of disasters from WW1 onwards culminated in the town's being devastated by an explosion in 1944 during the British evacuation, which also involved the people being forcibly evicted to Cyprus and then Australia.

By fifty years ago the population had declined to barely a hundred and most of the houses in Kastelorizo Town were in ruins. Its setting for the Oscar-winning film 'Mediterraneo' in the 90s and the Greek Government's concern that its further decay might see it taken over by Turkey, meant that a revival of sorts took place, further assisted by Australian emigrants returning to see or claim their heritage.

Like a less-developed Symi, its principal attraction is the deep bay of the harbour, once bordered by rows of grand mansions; far less so today though the natural grandeur remains. As for sights, there's a ruined castle, hammam, an interesting museum housed in the mosque – and a Lycian tomb, built into the rock face round the point of the town headland.

Beyond that there's not a lot to do. A steep climb up the steps behind the town leads over the top to a monastery after about forty-five minutes. Or there are small taxi-boat trips to a well-designed beach area at Agios Georgios round the coast.

You won't even be stressed by the sad-looking groups of refugees, shipped over at night from Kas on the Turkish coast opposite, waiting for their onward transfer to mainland Greece. A lesson not to be too indulgent about your own petty fears.

Kastelorizo is, however, one of these islands where you'll be right to worry about missing the ferry on departure – the next one could be a week away (though there is an airport in the interior) In fact, as we were leaving, a couple appeared on the quay, looking imploringly at the departing vessel. Since hardly anywhere is more than a quarter of a mile from the ferry quay, missing the boat ought to be virtually impossible. Insouciant Greeks – bit of stereotyping there – often run things too close. But the myth that everything runs late in Greece is unlikely to deceive the nervous traveller.

After this diversion to the most easterly part of Greece, and returning to the northernmost part of the Dodecanese, a little further to the north brings you to three more islands that don't really belong in any group: Samos, Ikaria and Fourni.

Samos, Ikaria and Fourni

Samos

Almost as close to Turkey as Kastelorizo but far larger, Samos has a variety of attractive features though it has been badly affected by the refugee crisis – the evidence here might not be good for the nerves if you're in the wrong place. Mountainous and green, with extensive forests, it is good for walking.

The capital, Vathy, on the north of the island at the head of a deep bay, also has good short-walking opportunities over or round the hill behind it to Agios Paraskevi for lunch, a couple of hours each way. It has a good museum, with an impressive five metre-high kouros (Marble male figure).

Pythagorio (the birthplace of Pythagoras and re-named in his honour from its earlier, and perhaps more appropriate one of Tigani – frying pan) has a less dramatic setting than Vathy but some attractive features. These include the castle and, up the hill, the Efplanos tunnel, actually a thousand-metre-long aqueduct through the mountain, built in antiquity by the Tyrant Polykrates. A short section is open to visitors though – nerve alert –

after passing through a narrow slit at the entrance, it's rather claustrophobic inside.

A few kilometres west of Pythagorio is the archaeological site of the Heraion, dedicated to Hera, wife of Zeus, of whom Samos was reputedly the birthplace. This is on the road to the airport, about a forty-five-minute walk away.

A week could easily be whiled away on Samos, albeit organised walks would give you easier access to some of the opportunities, unless you just want to laze on one of the south-western beaches. Via Pythagorio, the airport used to provide onward travel to the northern Dodecanese islands but, since the only flights there now are from Gatwick, this option is much reduced.

From the port of Karlovassi on the north-west coast, ferries run to Fourni and Ikaria. As I flew into Ikaria (nerve-alert coming), I'll start with that one.

Ikaria

Viewed from the Greek mainland, Ikaria, out in the middle of the Aegean, seems in the middle of nowhere. This fact meant that from Byzantine times it was used as a place of exile and quite extensively so during the Civil War (1946-9) and the Colonels' Junta (1967-74) when many leading left-wing figures were exiled there, including the composer Mikis Theodorakis in 1946-7. These latter punishments backfired somewhat as the exiles nourished an already-bolshie island mentality and Ikaria continues to elect Communist deputies to the Greek Parliament.

Slightly smaller than Kos but with less than half its population and a fraction of its tourists, Ikaria is dominated by its long mountain spine, rising to over three thousand feet in places and exudes a strange charm. In antiquity it was famed for its wine and though its name makes a claim as the starting-point of the flight of Ikaros (he'd have had a fair trek to make it from Crete, where the Minotaur was based, in the first place), it really seems to derive from a Phoenician word for fish.

On the subject of flight, this where the first nerve-alert comes in. The flight from Athens on a propeller-driven plane (slightly larger than the Kassos vintage) takes about an hour and lands at the airport at the northern tip of the island – through a wind tunnel, ie a cutting in the hill leading to the runway. A rather rolling entry even though – unusually – there wasn't much wind. It's one of the places where return to Athens or delays leaving are not unknown (second nerve alert). Strangely, although I had a ticket for the return flight, I chose to go back by sea – because it gave me greater variety, you realise, not because of any fears (and anyway, the wind still had its say).

The capital, Agios Kirikos, is about twenty kilometres down the south coast from the airport and is a fairly low-key place, though the forested mountains behind and the views out to sea give it a dour attractiveness. A top floor, sea-view room at the excellent Pension Kastro, up a small hill at the northern edge of town, provides sensational views out to the Fourni archipelago and Mount Kerkis on Samos, besides Patmos on the far horizon. (The only nervous breakdown-inducing event here was a sudden loud, crashing sound in the middle of the night, which I thought was someone trying to smash the front door down. I needn't have worried – and the police station was only down the hill – it was the Blue

Star Myconos dropping and lifting its anchor in the port. Inconvenient ferry arrivals are another reason Ikaria is difficult to visit.)

So there's no great abundance of tourists, which could count as a bonus, if not for the islanders. Partly for this reason, eating places, other than bars and cafes, seem to be sparse: one tourist centre, though said to be past its best now, is the spa resort of Therma, a short walk away.

The main tourist resort on the island is Armenistis, on the north-west coast and about forty kilometres away by a road most guidebooks describe as 'hair-raising' or a terror ride, presumably aided by a macho taxi or bus driver (though buses are said to be rare on the island). Hang on, hang on, a bit of judicious nervousness can help here. Purely by chance, when I first arrived, a woman taxi driver took me from the airport to Agios Kirikos so I engaged her to take me to Armenistis and, while the road certainly winds, up as high as two thousand feet, it was completely relaxing. (A taxi from Rafina to Athens airport, by contrast, is more like an F1 race).

The route passes through Evdilos, also on the north coast and the island's second port, which guidebooks tend to enthuse about. If you're stuck in its narrow main street, it is reminiscent of a Cornwall seaside village. A lorry caused major, if brief, paralysis (not mine this time).

Armenistis is an amenable little place, spreading uphill from its harbour. The tasteful Hotel Erofili – with a quote from Kazantzakis on the wall on the way to the pool, always a good sign – has glorious views across the bay to the two extensive, nearby beaches and, looking further north, even a glimpse of Samos, while to the left can be seen the small harbour. The taverna Pascalia had excellent food (best soutsoukakia since 2001) and open red wine, with an outdoor terrace above the sea.

There are plenty of walking opportunities on Ikaria, though perhaps more for the adventurous, if going off into the countryside. A short – four kilometres – road walk from Armenistis brings you to Nas, again lauded by guidebooks, partly for the one archaeological site of any note – a shrine to Artemis – and partly for the rocky cove nearby: a long trek down – and back up.

A more interesting road walk is uphill towards the so-called Rahes villages, a scattering of four, of which Agios Dimitrios is the first you come to. As the road winds upwards, wonderful vistas open of the sea through the pines. At one point a sign indicated a 'round of Rahes' trail but it said three hours and I didn't have the time (no, not the nerve, what a hurtful suggestion). The Rahes villages are said to be where the people sleep all day and live through the night. Naturally wary of this sort of thing, I didn't linger, though the one person I did speak to, popping up, improbably, from under an upturned boat (at a thousand feet?) not only spoke excellent English but was concerned to know if I was lost.

A frequent visitor to the island told me of a bizarre legacy of the Treaty of Lausanne (1923) that forbids the Greeks to station arms there. As a result, Turkish fighters make frequent over-flights, secure in the knowledge they can't be shot down.

Ikaria deserves more exploring, for which a car is probably necessary, though it's not something I'd enjoy: someone I met claimed to have driven on every road on the island. I did, however, make three boat trips while there, the last to leave the island.

You'll recall earlier that I'd decided not simply to fly back to Athens but to return by ferry, via Syros and Tinos, to Rafina. This was partly due to the discovery that, five days into my trip, there was actually an afternoon ferry departure from Agios Kirikos, across to Mykonos and thence to Syros on its way to Piraeus.

The 'Blue Star Myconos' was, of course, three quarters of an hour late, but then it had started from Lemnos at nine the previous evening. By four pm the wind had got up and actually crossing the gangway to board was an uneasy experience, with a not-unreasonable fear of being blown off. The voyage down the south coast of Ikaria was blowy, the ship already rolling. When we passed the southern tip and headed west, the blow increased and started to throw spray up as high as Deck 8. It was time to retreat indoors and huddle in a lounge while the horizon rose and fell through the misted windows. I've since read that the stretch of the Aegean between Ikaria and Mykonos is the windiest of the whole sea. No disagreement from here.

The other two boat trips enabled a day visit to Fourni, an hour's sailing from Agios Kirikos. Guidebooks had suggested that caiques made this regular trip, but information was predictably thin on the ground. When I asked at a travel agent's that was said to sell tickets, they pointed me to the agency at the other end of the street. This appeared derelict. However, on the Sunday morning, having gone down to the waterfront for breakfast, I noticed activity on the nearby quay, close to a small boat.

Wandering round there, I asked a port policeman if trips to Fourni had finished. No! The boat was coming. But did I have a ticket? Cue panic. He pointed me to an agency along the street from the one I'd assumed I'd been directed to previously. Cue dash and more panic, as they seemed to be taking ages over dispensing tickets to the two people ahead of me. This was partly from the fact that they were computerised ferry tickets – no caique, then? The little boat I'd seen turned out to be a fishing boat – and partly from the need to complete a Covid boarding form.

Palpitations thumping, I dashed back to the quay. The small car ferry 'Megalochari' was still some way off – panic unnecessary, as usual. The outward journey was a bit blustery, with occasional spray over the open top deck but all good fun. Calling first at the other (just) inhabited island, Thimena, the ferry then deposited me at

Fourni

Fourni is another island that had intrigued me and I'd toyed with the idea of a package, but the complications of getting there deterring me. The lack of flights to Samos from the Midlands completed the job. Mainly centred on the port village of the same name, Fourni is a pleasant little place, though the surrounding hills give it a slightly closed-in feel. The main street, again rather narrower than expected, running inland up to a small square is, however, tree-lined and attractive.

While there's not a huge amount to do – a walk up the hill past the beach gives good views over Thimena and the beach is a rather scruffy, pebbly affair – as a day-trip destination it offers far more than Arki or even Lipsi. There are good fish tavernas on the front – Fourni is the centre of the fishing industry in the central Aegean – and up by the square there was an unobtrusive taverna selling fresh calamares, together with local horta and cheerful hospitality. An empty Roman sarcophagus provided the only antiquity of note.

With more time you could take in a hop over to Thimena or wander out to remote beaches past Kambi. No hardship for the nerves.

Going on north from these islands you're into the

NORTH-EAST AEGEAN

Again, not the most accessible from the UK unless you live in the south-east or like dicing with Smart motorways ('There's a no-no for the nervous driver). As a result, Chios, the next one north, and Lemnos and Samothace, beyond, remain on the unlikely-to-do list, as does Skyros out in the central Aegean since first you have to cross Evia for the ferry connexion. A pity because both Lemnos and Skyros have links with the Gallipoli campaign in 1915, Skyros being where Rupert Brooke is buried. So the next island to cover is:

LESVOS

The third largest Greek island, Lesvos (how it ever managed to be called Lesbos given that the Greek is clearly V just confirms western ignorance) has suffered hugely from the Syrian refugee crisis – or rather the failure of the EU to support Greece in coping with it, thanks largely to widespread xenophobia and prejudice, especially from the members whose historical record during the Third Reich has clearly not been forgotten by swathes of their populations. Italy and

Greece have grudgingly soldiered on, with some support from Spain and contributions from much of northern Europe (largely excluding us).

However, the toll on Lesvos (and Samos) in particular, has been heavy with an initial degree of welcome from the island's population – and Greece had its own refugee crisis in the 1920s following the catastrophe on the Turkish mainland – turning to anger and worse as they were overwhelmed by the numbers and lack of provision.

Obviously, your nerves may make you steer clear of Lesvos (though the lack of UK flights is just as likely to be the cause), but if you risk it, it has much to offer.

To some extent an island of two halves, since the Gulf of Kalloni makes a deep incision through its centre, Lesvos is really a holiday island – somewhat ironically in the current climate, although historically it was not that dependent on tourism.

The north-western town of Molyvos, an attractive place dominated by its castle, is a major resort on the western half of the island, providing a wide range of amenities, and tourism hasn't ruined its appearance or ambience.

Lesvos is an island with literary connexions, most famously to the female poet of antiquity, Sappho, whose legend has probably been distorted in the loss of much of her output. The pleasant south-western beach resort of Skala Eressou claims kinship as she was born nearby, though you'll need a car to reach it.

Less well-known in western Europe is the important twentieth-century Greek novelist Stratis Myrivilis (1892-1969), born in Sykaminia, about twenty kilometres east of Molyvos. The small seaside village/fishing port below it,

Skala Sykaminias, provides the setting for one of his major novels, translated into English as 'The Mermaid Madonna'.

You can have coffee under the huge plane tree in the square that features in the novel and admire the chapel on the rock that has a similar importance – where it's known as the Chapel of the Madonna, though, as I've noted of Leros previously, its scale in the novel dwarfs the reality.

Among two other of Myrivilis' novels available in English are 'The Schoolmistress with the Golden Eyes', the first section of which depicts the appalling horrors of the Greek attempt to take Anatolia back from Turkey in 1921 and the disaster that followed, culminating in the burning and destruction of Smyrna the following year. (While modern Turks attribute that atrocity –completely disingenuously – to the retreating Greek army, Myrivilis' work suggests that the Turkish reprisals were not without basis in fact).

The other, 'Life in the Tomb', depicts the fighting on the largely forgotten front at Salonika in WW1, a campaign in which Myrivilis also took part. Again, an unflinching portrait of the suffering and futility of war, it had a wide readership in Greece in the 1920s.

Happier times may see Lesvos able to show off its attractions in the future, though it's not a prospect that looks imminent.

Skipping on past Lemnos, the final island I've visited in the north-eastern Aegean, and a dozen kilometres south of the northern Greek coastline, is

THASSOS

The most northerly inhabited Greek island (the uninhabited islet to the north, Thassopoula, claims the ultimate accolade) and mainly a holiday island, since there are no ferry connexions to anywhere to the south, making island-hopping from there an impossibility, Thassos is an attractive destination, with a good deal of archaeological interest. With a mountainous interior – the highest peak is over three thousand feet – it is also very green, with extensive forests but, as the most northerly, it does get more rain than the stereotypical Greek island – hence all the greenery – so, if you're after a holiday in the sun, you could be unlucky.

Thassos is most easily reached by flights into Kavala, followed by a short bus ride to the port of Keramoti for the thirty-five-minute ferry crossing to Limenas/Thassos Town. There's often an hour's wait in Keramoti which allows time for a Greek salad beside the sea as an introduction to Greece after the flight. Nerves evaporate!

Limenas abounds with archaeological remains: the Agora, Odeon (closed), Arch of Caracalla, Temple of Dionysos and Sanctuary of Hercules (cut by the road and with excavations all over the place) are all within the town itself, while the Theatre (in 1997 a sign said it was closed until 2000, you may be lucky now) is a short way out, close to the impressive walls. The Theatre can be viewed from higher up the hill, its chief feature being the trees growing out of some of the rows of seats.

The massive City walls, dating from 4BC, circle the town and are in varying states of repair. It's possible to follow them round, often alongside. A path leads from the Theatre through the woods up to the Acropolis, later incorporated into a medieval kastro. From there, still following the walls, on a circular walk that brings you back into the town, you come to the remains of a Temple of Athena, with good views over the town, then a shrine to Pan and several of the City gates.

A bus follows the coastal road to give a tour of the island but, from Limenas, a short walk along the path through pine woods, brings you to Makriyiannos, while an hour and a half's road walking south, via the impressive Selinus Gate and passing a disused marble quarry, reaches Panagia, often described as an attractive hillside village but too big to be that appealing.

Since frequent hydrofoils sail from Limenas to Kavala, a forty-five-minute crossing, an easy day trip is possible. Kavala has a relaxed atmosphere and several sites of historical interest. The Turkish quarter, to the east of the harbour, has an impressive aqueduct now spanning more modern houses, a number of old buildings and is overlooked by the shell of a Byzantine castle. The site of the Battle of Philippi, where Mark Antony defeated Brutus and Cassius, the murderers of Julius Caesar, in 42AD, lies 15km north of the city and is said to be well-preserved. Unfortunately, I couldn't make sense of the bus timetables so was too nervous to try it: another missed opportunity.

The other failure of my nerve was not taking the chance of a day-trip to Samothrace. I saw an advert for such a jaunt, by hydrofoil the following Sunday, but decided I wasn't sure about hydrofoil toilets – well, they were built for Russian lake travel and with the wind out in the northern Aegean… They say that it's the things you *don't* do that you regret most!

Otherwise Thassos has enough elements for a stress-free stay.

SPORADES ISLANDS

SPORADES

From Thassos the only way is south and the first string of islands, though a couple of hundred kilometres distant, are the Sporades, the scattered islands, off the coast of the Pelion peninsula, the main three of which are Skiathos, Skopelos and Alonissos. Although Pelion is not an island, its attractiveness and comparative lack of intrusive development mean it deserves inclusion in this guide.

SKIATHOS

As the nearest to the mainland, Skiathos is the first you come to, not least because all three islands are served by its airport, though there is a seasonal boat link from Platanos in the southern Pelion or you could come by ferry from Volos. Given that flights from UK regional airports to Volos are rarer than those to the moon and then travelling down the length of Pelion more difficult still, you can see why Skiathos airport is convenient.

The most heavily-touristed of the Sporades, Skiathos has fine beaches and the wooded interior helps avoid too great a sense of over-development. Skiathos Town is only a few minutes from the airport (avoid too-close sightseeing when a plane is taking off: there are records of tourists doing an involuntary Icarus-without-wings off the end of the runway when they tried it: nervous stress will be the least of your worries) and nestles behind an islet-littered bay. Its waterfront is bustling, both with boats and ferries, and rows of tavernas and cafes that manage to avoid being too raucous, in daytime, at least.

If you're going on to one of the other islands, you may get the opportunity to sample Skiathos, either when waiting for the ferry or, if your transfer bus comes down the hill from the airport just in time to see the last hydrofoil disappearing between the offshore islets, a night on the island. While the latter is unlikely to give you the chance to sample the lively night-life – too expensive for a tour company, rooms along the coast that are reminiscent of a set for 'Beau Geste' are more likely, though interesting enough – there may be a further bonus. You'll recall my trepidation on Thassos about hydrofoils (see above). If you have to stay overnight on Skiathos, there's a good chance that the next morning you'll make the transfer on a real boat! Not only that, it could do a circuit round the northern coast of Skopelos so you have a round-the-island tour thrown in.

This did, indeed, happen en route to

SKOPELOS

The largest of the Sporades and much quieter than Skiathos, Skopelos is one of the islands that has no airport because it chose not to: holding on to its forests and avoiding mass tourism proved to be a wise move. Although filming of some of the key scenes of the film 'Mama Mia' here has brought more tourism in the years since, its effect has not been obtrusive (and, in fact quite useful – see below. That the sequel was filmed in Bulgaria – cheaper, no doubt – has also helped).

The 'Express Skiathos', a catamaran/car ferry duly headed first for Loutraki, the port for (and known on ferry timetables as) Glossa, Skopelos' second town, perched on the hill some way above. Then it was off round the north of the island and down the east coast to the main town and port, Skopelos Town. Attractively set against a hill around a wide bay, Skopelos Town has a sedate charm and retains much of its traditional feel in the Old Town. One kafenion on the waterfront behind the old port sells only Greek coffee and good stuff at that (the Mama Mia café on the beach road had clearly been defunct for some time).

A series of tavernas front the same beach road, ranging from the Skiathos-type-and-price to the more traditional – Stou Dimitriakou being of the latter and exceptional.

Short walks are possible in either direction from the town. Following the beach road (on which there's a small archaeological site) the route winds uphill towards a couple of monasteries. On the other side of town, climbing up (and up – it's steep) through the Old Town and then following the road brings you down to Glifoneri beach, with a good taverna. A longer walk, partly following the old road, leads to the beach at Stafilos and passes an hospitable café called 'Rosemary' on the main road, authentically Greek, and specialising in small pies. The island walking guide has this route, though it wasn't over-clear (can't remember if an alternative title for *this* book was the 'Dim traveller'). The beach at Stafilos, dropping down steeply from a side road, is pretty. As it's on the bus route, return that way, rather than repeating the 4km walk, is possible.

An island coach tour, now re-branded as the Mama Mia Tour (and not as naff as it might sound), is a useful way of seeing more of the island without having to hire a car. It drives through the wooded centre of the island (whereas the local bus follows the coast road) before turning off towards the east coast to the small church of Agios Ioannis, high on a spur of rock above the sea and scene of the wedding in the film. With a car you'd be too nervous to manage the winding, narrow road – think of meeting a tour coach. There are 220 steps up to the tiny church, which required a larger façade for the film and, as the interior holds about ten people, the interior scenes in the film were actually shot at Shepperton Studios. Still, the church is well worth seeing in its own right – and it does have a toilet. As that's at the back on the edge of the cliff, this may not be as reassuring as you'd hope.

The tour then proceeds to Glossa, visiting an interesting olive oil factory (a giveaway to the tour's antecedents) before stopping at Kastani Beach, another film location that has been tastefully developed since as a small beach resort. Finally, you stop at Agnondas for lunch. Again, not a film location, Agnondas has, however, a delightful setting beside the sea and actually also serves as an alternative port to Skopelos Town which, being north-facing, is sometimes rendered inaccessible to ferries by strong winds.

Skopelos is a graceful island without being wildly dramatic or exciting (good for the nerves), nor is it much of an island-hopper's destination, since onward travel ends at the next island along (although some guides suggest periodic ferries run to Evia and Skyros, don't bank on it):

Alonissos

Aligned north-east whereas Skopelos was aligned north-west, Alonissos is also narrower than the other two and is known for its clear waters, partly due to its isolation and partly to its being in a National Marine Park. Also in the Marine Park are several smaller islands, largely uninhabited.

Being at the end of the line, a day trip from one of the other islands is unlikely to get you there before midday and the last ferry usually leaves about four pm. If you access the island by hydrofoil, they can be crowded and roll about in the wind. Stress alert? Probably means you need to stay a while to calm the nerves.

The main town/port (well, the only one really), Patitiri, sits at the south of the island and a 1965 earthquake means there's little architectural heritage. The island's Hora, above Patitiri, was similarly affected by the earthquake but has good views and there's both a bus service up there and a path down (if you can find the start), with plentiful taxis doing the five-minute journey (the walk down takes forty). Just to the north of Patitiri is Roussoum Beach (though lacking shade) and Votsi, almost an extension of Patitiri and with a pleasant beach. An Anavasi map shows a number of slightly longer walks, mainly through pine forests, though the north of Alonissos is fairly barren. You may need a car to reach the start points.

Boat trips form a large part of the activities around the island. A major one goes north through the channel between

Alonissos and its adjacent, uninhabited neighbour, Peristera, out to Kyra Panaghia, where you can disembark and walk up the steep steps and path to the monastery, looked after in 2000 by one monk. Further north and west, the islands of Gioura and Piperi can be viewed but are off-limits to landing in order to protect the monk seals and other endangered species.

Another boat trip heads east to the island of Skandzoura, though this can be cancelled due to wind (in which case, you can breathe a sigh of relief at not being caught out in it), while a shorter one, often dressed up as a sunset cruise, takes in the islet of Agios Giorgios in the channel between Alonissos and Skopelos. Landing is possible, with a short, steep ascent up to the now-abandoned monastery. The trip gives good views up the cliffs to Hora as well as the sunset over Skopelos.

Scuba diving is a popular activity on Alonissos but it's obviously not something for the nervous traveller.

As you'll have calmed down considerably after a stay in the Sporades, I can now let slip the intriguing book about them, published in 1965 and by Michael Carroll, called originally 'Gates of the Wind', that apparently being Greek fisherman's term for the area. (Now I tell you). Since re-titled 'An Island in Greece: on the Shores of Skopelos', either (a) because modern ferries (and, er, hydrofoils?) have tamed the winds or (b) there are too many nervous travellers around.

It's time to turn to a bit of dry land:

PELION

O r, as Michael Carroll's map has it, the Magnesian Promontory. The hook-shaped peninsula on the mainland to the west of the Sporades, Pelion – or Pilio in Greek – while clearly not an island, is so enticing and beautiful it deserves to be, and has sea on three sides anyway so it almost counts as one. It does here. And, as indicated above, deserves its inclusion. If you don't like that, go to Halki. This isn't a Guide for the Pedantic Traveller.

The landscape is varied, the north, with Mount Pelion (home of the mythical Centaurs – I said mythical, you're in no danger) rising to five thousand feet, and the area having rich fruit-growing areas and extensive forests; while the southern section has lower hills rolling down to the sea. It is an excellent area for walking, though to make the most of its opportunities, a guided walking trip is advisable (HF Holidays, based at Horto on the west coast, is first-rate).

In 2000, flights from the UK landed in Volos but in the recent past the arrival airport (for HF certainly) has been Thessaloniki, a three-and-a half-hour coach transfer away – not as bad as it sounds and certainly not stressful because much of the journey is on good motorway (with views of Mount Olympos) and a pleasant service area about halfway provides a welcome break.

On the north-east coast Agios Ioannis is an attractive seaside resort below high wooded hills. Pods of dolphins swimming north are a not-infrequent sight. One impressive longish walk heads south from Agios Ioannis past the beach of Papanero and the hamlet of Damouchari and then up a long kalderimi, with spectacular views, to the dispersed village of Tsangarada. One of its quarters, Agia Paraskevi, features a huge plane tree reputed to be a thousand years old.

Walks directly inland (and uphill) lead to Mouresi and Kissos but are mainly on road (well, for a nervous traveller, they are) and in the forest it's often difficult to know exactly where you are. (Only on the coach transfer back to Volos did I realise that the taverna I was unable to find a few days previously had been a couple of bends in the road further up). This wasn't a guided walk trip so naturally my range was limited and I got lost a couple of times, but the path up to Tsangarada proved addictive and roadside fountains dispense gloriously cold drinking-water.

Southern Pelion was visited on an HF guided walking trip, as mentioned above. The village of Horto, on the east coast, looking over the Pagasitic Gulf towards the mountains of Magnesia on the mainland, is in the less populated sector of the peninsula. Backed by rolling, wooded hills, it has fine views over the gulf, and glorious sunsets. Even the flashes of lightning (infrequent, don't worry) across the Gulf are impressive. And Martha's Taverna has a deservedly high reputation.

Walks from Horto are plentiful, with transport to the start/finish. Most of these have been developed by local groups, who also provide a walking guide to the area. From Milina, a coastal village three kilometres south, a circular walk leads up in the hills via Lafkos, a pretty mountain hamlet; an easy ascent of around a thousand feet.

A couple of walks start further south and centre on Trikkeri, a hill village atop the hook of the peninsula. From Kottes on the western shore, a path leads up to Trikkeri, a good spot for a taverna lunch, then down to Agia Kyriaki, at the narrow entrance to the Gulf and with views of both the mainland and the northern bulk of Evia. A longer walk starts at the tip of the peninsula's claw, opposite the islet of Palia Trikkeri, another place with a grim history as a prison island. This walk reaches Trikkeri by following the ridge.

Another walk ends at Platanias on the south coast, directly facing Evia. This walk starts at Plomiri, an inland village. Only the section which passes below the (fenced off) property of the Colonel (no relation?), from which his vicious-looking dogs bark loudly through the fence, is likely to stir the nerves (well, shred them, more like. The comfort of a group helps. As would a gun).

To the north, from Argalasti, the major town of the area and inland, a circular walk descends to Kalamos, takes you along the shore to Pauo then fairly steeply uphill via a monastery (closed but with a nearby spring) back to Argalasti.

Probably the highlight walk starts further north again, inland of one of the major resorts, Kala Nera, and from the village of Vizitsa, preserved as a so-called 'traditional village', though tastefully so. A woman's co-operative operates a shop selling their excellent range of local delicacies. The smells and sights as you wind your way down to Milies, our destination, are fabulous (a longer track takes you down to the coast at Kala Nera, but omitting Milies would be a loss). The penultimate stretch of the walk to Milies follows the track of the still-operating section of a narrow-gauge railway line that used to start at Volos. (No, don't panic, it only operates now at weekends and anyway you'd hear it coming. A far more worrying bit is where the track crosses a narrow ravine. Oops. Just don't look down).

Milies, at the end of the line, has a restored station and a memorial to yet another massacre by occupying Germans in WW2. From the station there's a short, steep climb up to the village, with a large, shaded square, above which is a stunning little church. With small windows high up to avoid scrutiny from the then-occupying Turks, its interior is a glorious panoply of colour – walls covered with icons and gold at the front. Its acoustics are also intriguing: upturned jugs set into the ceiling and channels under the floor to allow for flowing water. And it even managed to avoid being despoiled by the various occupying powers. (They've now gone, you can calm down)

Evia has been mentioned – and seen – on a few occasions from Pelion (and elsewhere, to follow) and would be the next island south were it not for the fact that Covid has repeatedly proved a deterrent. So, the islands next to cover are in the Northern Cyclades, with the first you reach to the south being Andros.

THE CYCLADES ISLANDS

ANDROS

The second-largest and most northerly of the Cyclades, Andros is green and hilly, with the odd mountain and offers plenty of opportunities for walking in attractive countryside. Reached by fairly frequent ferries from Rafina, the second port of Athens – half an hour by bus from the airport – its one main port is Gavrion on the west coast, while the capital, Hora lies further south across the island on the east coast. The principal resort is Batsi, eight kilometres down the coast.

Hora is an attractive town, set on a narrow spit of land in a wide bay, though north-facing, so vulnerable to wind. With many impressive houses, it also has a couple of museums though, if you ever find the naval museum open, put out a major alert.

There are plenty of walking routes inland from Batsi, with paths – often goat tracks – leading left and right off the river-bed and along the road to Katakilos. A so-called Albanian road, of some age, also provides a route up into the hills. Inland from Gavrion, a circular walk will pass a strange

Hellenistic tower – with the chance of seeing peregrine falcons trying to deter a buzzard from attacking their nest in it, a monastery and camomile terraces. Taking the bus further south from Batsi to the pretty village of Paleopoli, you can walk down the 1039 steps to the ancient site of Paleopoli near (and under) the beach. Elaborate dovecotes can be seen on the way and after climbing the steps back up, return to Batsi is along the road, then via the beaches.

Guided walks may be available to enable you to see some of the pretty inland villages, since the bus service doesn't penetrate far from the main road. On such a walk all sorts of fruit tree will be encountered – fig, pomegranate, mulberry, peach, lemon etc, a profusion of richness. So, all should be stress-free.

From Andros it is easy to make a day-trip to the next island south and separated from it by a narrow channel,

TINOS

A sedate and, except for the two major religious festivals in March and August, tranquil island, the interior of Tinos is really accessible only by car. Although there are many villages, the bulk of the population lives in Tinos Town, also the main port and dominated, first by the elaborate church of Panagia Evangelistria and, further inland, the conical peak of Mount Exoburgo which, at nearly two thousand feet, is visible for miles around.

The new port, with pleasant cafes on the elevated road behind to enable waiting for your ferry in comfort and with clear views of its approach, is a short walk along the front from the agreeably bustling town waterfront. This curves round a crescent-shaped bay to a raised headland. Just before the headland, the road turns left and runs down the south coast of the island, passing beaches such as Agios Fokas, with shade from tamarisk trees, some sandy stretches and a number of tavernas, with views across to Delos, Mykonos and Syros.

Tinos Town is a friendly place to spend some time. If your nerves are bad – or your conscience is – the standard penance here is to make the ascent up to the church – on your knees. If I remember correctly, there's a strip of red carpet, probably of some durable nylon material, that you can follow all the way (it's separated from the traffic by cones so the chances of being bowled over by a passing car are remote). The pilgrimage may not soothe your nerves (or conscience) but the pain in your knees will take your mind off them.

The calm atmosphere on Tinos could make arrival at the next island south, and end of the ferry line, something of a culture shock:

MYKONOS

Small, heavily-touristed and a magnet for all kinds of excess, Mykonos is probably best visited for its easy access to Delos (ah, at last), unless you're into self-display and bling-shopping. The port/town has its photogenic aspects – the houses overhanging the sea, the odd windmill and the pelicans – and the winding, narrow streets of the old town are much-touted, but there are several elsewhere of greater appeal – Naxos, the Hora on Amorgos and Rhodes old town, among others. That aside, the accommodation office just off the quay in the Old Port is very helpful.

The usual inconvenience is that Mykonos has two ports and the newer, Tourlos, is 2.5 km to the north. Buying a ferry ticket requires clarification as to which port your ferry will use. Your nerves will be too frayed by now to care anyway.

The town beach in the harbour from which Delos tour boats depart struck me as scruffy but it was full of Americans saying 'Gee, isn't this amazing.'

Now, before your nervous anticipation bursts, it's off on a day-trip to:

DELOS

The birthplace of Apollo and Artemis, the small island of Delos became the centre of the Delian League and its treasury following the Persian wars, so both a spiritual and commercial centre. In order to preserve the former, giving birth or being buried on the island was banned and the population was moved to neighbouring Rinia. Once Athens usurped the role of Delos and removed the treasures, it fell into decline, though revived enough later to become the biggest slave market in the Mediterranean. Even later still it became the model for Rishi Sunak's freeport scheme in 2021. (Reasons no doubt to do with the spiritual)

Nowadays Delos, mainly flat with only the small hill of Mount Kynthos having any elevation, is just a large archaeological site and the short boat trip from Mykonos gives about four hours on the island (could put the bladder under stress). All good guidebooks provide a layout of the site (That why there isn't one here?) – 'Greek Island Hopping' has an excellent map and an extensive commentary. It also suggests covering the site in an anti-clockwise direction since that means you ascend Mount Kynthos early in the trip. (I went up twice as I managed to leave 'Greek Island Hopping' at the top – can't think what I was doing to put it down.)

You might find yourself bemused by the profusion of jumbled stone. However, you're unlikely to miss the theatre, the Sacred Lake (drained in the 20s to deter mosquitos) or the famous lions nearby, though the five survivors of a once-extensive row are plaster replicas, the originals being in the museum. Sculpted without manes, they do look rather mangy and underwhelming. So would you be after two thousand years.

The museum has a wealth of exhibits but tends to be crowded and, especially after wandering round the site in the sun, you're likely to be feeling a bit overwhelmed. Then there are the toilets. (Inside, in 'Greek Island Hopping's plan but I could have sworn they were outside. Maybe I missed something.)

If you're not worrying about that, and whether you'll get back to the port in order not to miss the boat, you could give some thought to the fact there are supposed to be plenty of snakes around. As long as you're not in bare feet (as if a nervous traveller would be), you'll be OK. And they're small anyway. So I've read.

The Cyclades derive their name from circling Delos so better head north-west to

SYROS

The administrative capital of the Cyclades, Syros is a small island, roughly the same size as Mykonos but with more than three times the permanent population. As with Tinos, my knowledge of it is restricted to the main town, Ermoupolis, on the east coast, built round an imposing natural harbour and guarded by two cathedral-topped hills (one Catholic, one Orthodox). Much of the rest of the island, especially the north, is barren and arid, though there are a few beaches in the south. However, the island has a relaxed feel (note) and people tend to speak favourably about its refined attributes. Recently, an expat pointed out that the north has an extensive series of peaceful walking trails.

A working town, on arrival you are first struck by the huge Neorian shipyard on your left. From the busy waterfront, backed by a warren of pedestrianised narrow streets, elegant buildings run inland to Miaoulis Square and then you proceed on and up to the Catholic cathedral above the quarter of Ano Syros.

With ferry links to a number of islands – I came once from Kea and more recently from Ikaria (the ferry on its way up to Piraeus) – Syros provides a restful stopping-off point for island-hopping. Its appeal shouldn't be underestimated.

Circling anti-clockwise from Syros means heading further northwest, with views of the barren, uninhabited, former prison island of Giaros, before coming to

KEA

Although one of the closest islands to the mainland, Kea is not the easiest to get to, at least for foreign tourists. Ferries depart from Lavrion: from the airport you have to get a bus to Markopoulo, fifteen minutes away, wait for half an hour for the bus from Athens and then pass through the Attica countryside for another hour. A guidebook indicated that the ferry ticket office was in the town; it turned out to be on the quay. The ferry crossing is only a further hour and passes the notorious island of Makronisi, a now-uninhabited former penal location, most recently used during the Colonels' Junta (1967-74). It's said that people on the mainland could hear, at night, the cries of the tortured. Remains of the buildings are visible and there's an almost palpable feeling of evil (no, this isn't the guide for the Tremulous Traveller).

As the ferry traverses the Kea Channel, another historical association from the not-quite-so-recent past lurks below: the wreck of the Titanic's sister ship, 'Britannic', which struck a mine on its way, as a hospital ship, to the Dardanelles in 1915. Although it was therefore empty of patients, thirty or so people were killed when two of its lifeboats were caught in the still-turning propellers. (Don't worry, there've been no reported sightings of mines recently. Mind you, this one was apparently floating below the surface so you can still feel nervous. Pity I mentioned either of these features really.)

Another curiosity from this trip – one of several – was that as we were disembarking a little girl asked me if I was a 'kapetanios'. This was the Greek term for Civil War communist resistance fighters. When I said I was English she looked even more puzzled.

Kea is one of the few islands where arrival is not greeted by hordes of people offering rooms. The main port, Korissia, is a low-key affair, which doesn't go overboard to advertise its wares. In fact, you have to hunt for a room: many of the Greek visitors have property on the island.

There is, apparently, a bus service from Korissia to the capital, Ioulis, but with the absence of any timetable or bus stop, it remained elusive. Ioulis was, however, walkable in little more than an hour (uphill). Ioulis itself is an attractive place, set in a bowl of the hills and with narrow streets. It also has an excellent museum, which reflects the Minoan past, including a striking selection of large-breasted women, similar to those found at Knossos and elsewhere on Crete, but in red clay.

There are a number of marked and numbered walking paths on Kea. Path 1 passes the Lion of Kea, a 6BC stone carving, on the way down to Otzias on the north coast.

Of the further curiosities of Kea encountered on this pleasant walk, much of it down a tree-lined dry stream-bed, one was the prevalence of spiders' webs stretched across the path, many at head height (Don't panic, you're unlikely to get caught. And a walking pole comes in handy here.) Another was that, at one point, I found myself walking for several minutes in a cloud of butterflies. Enchanting. (One alternative title for this book was 'Walking with Butterflies' but it doesn't have the same frisson – or lack of taste – as 'toilets'.)

A final curiosity was that on my last night on Kea the ground floor room I was in was covered in small beetles by the morning. They didn't appear to be able to climb far but on each of the next two islands one dropped out of my rucksack.

So Kea can be recommended as an island slightly out-of-the-ordinary and certainly not despoiled by mass tourism. A relief after the nerves stretched on the way.

The next island south, Kythnos, is still on the to-do list: for some reason its ferry connexions are not that good and guide books tend to stress its lack of attractions, although Sunvil recently began offering not only packages there but also guided walking options. So, the next island to focus on is

SERIFOS

Serifos is a small but attractive island, like many of the southern Cyclades with a fairly barren interior. However, there is more greenery around the port, Livadi, which is set at the head of a deeply-indented bay on the southeast coast. It most distinctive feature is the Hora, perched on a rocky pinnacle a pleasant two-kilometre walk up from Livadi and with steep stairways to the views from the top of the upper town. Beyond Hora, tracks fan out up the mountain into small, isolated settlements or, more generally, into the back of beyond. Rambling, if you have no particular place to go or hurry to get there, is probably a relaxing occupation. Take plenty of water.

In fact, relaxing is the main activity on Serifos, with a number of good beaches and beachfront tavernas stretching out from Livadi. The nerves should have a rest. Had you been here in antiquity, of course, that may not have been so easy. The island is where Perseus returned with the head of the Gorgon – whose gaze could turn you to stone – and used it to wreak revenge on the king and many of his subjects for their treatment of his mother. While the head is unlikely still to be lying around, if you do stumble across one covered in snakes, look away quickly before… No, don't cross Serifos off your list, it's really a pleasant place to visit.

I couldn't say the same for the next island south,

SIFNOS

It began well. I found a pleasant room in the main port, Kamares, set in a wide bay on the north-west coast, the room with lemon blossom over the terrace. Sifnos is slightly bigger than Serifos and with twice the population (a couple of thousand). A rich island in antiquity because of gold deposits, it has a more refined feel (not necessarily an advantage) and an extensive bus network (if bussing about is to your taste).

It also has plenty of walking trails though, in 2002, I can't say I stumbled on any. (Yes, I know. Dim Traveller again). From the capital, Apollonia, I wandered about the nearby hills, to Ano Petali and Artemos, scenic though none seemed very dramatic; return to Kamares was along a fairly busy road.

So what put me off? Trivia. The Alpha Bank in Apollonia charged me five percent commission for changing some traveller's cheques (its advertised rate was 1.5) and in a shop in Kamares I was blatantly short-changed (probably of one euro).

OK, OK, but when you're a nervous traveller, these things can knock you off balance. I stayed two nights on Sifnos, went up to Serifos and then returned in order to get a boat across to Paros the following Sunday: as indicated previously, the ferry lines run out from Piraeus like the spokes in a wheel and crossing from one spoke to the next is virtually impossible – who but some idiot island-hopper would ever want such a facility?(Yes, this is The Stupid Trav…) – so this was a rare opportunity not to be missed. (Greek has no simple equivalent for 'island hopping', which says a lot).

The first shock on returning to Kamares was discovering that this ferry to Paros didn't leave from there but from Faros on the opposite side of the island. Did I panic? (You have the cheek to ask?) Remember the good bus service. This did, naturally, involve changing buses at Apollonia, so more nerve-rattling, but I was deposited in Faros in good time. Enough in fact for a pleasant lunch overlooking the bay before departing on the 'Antiparos Express', a rather grand title for what was a caique.

Still, I was on my way and nerves surviving.

Although Paros was my next destination from Serifos the next island south on this anti-clockwise circuit of the Cyclades is

MILOS

As in Venus de. Another island I didn't quite get on with. (Could it be me?) Milos, shaped like a piece from a jigsaw puzzle with the deep bay of Adamas, the main port, cut into the middle, is a volcanic leftover and the most southerly of the western Cyclades. For this reason the journey from Piraeus can take forever but in 2002 it was served by a direct link on Highspeed 3, which managed Milos in four hours.

Milos confirmed my abandonment, foreshadowed the previous year on Santorini, of camping in the Greek islands. A battered minibus met the ferry at Adamas and made the short journey round the bay to the site. It was a fair size but there was only one other tent. Maybe the fact that it rained for an hour as soon as I'd put the tent up (with flysheet the wrong way round) didn't help. Or standing in the toilet block for the hour until it stopped. Or the surrounding landscape: it wasn't exactly a moonscape, but opencast mining hadn't done a great deal for the attractiveness of this part of the island. Nor were the French-style foot-bath-type toilets a consolation.

Dinner in the site's taverna proved to be unexciting, too. Well, depressing. Limited choice (hard pasta) and lack of atmosphere hardly encouraged a long stay. What finished me off was the night. The one other tent, about a hundred yards away, turned out to belong to some Irish people. I only know that from their voices. They weren't making a great deal of noise, merely talking. Until 3am. Ear plugs had no effect. I'd had enough.

Next morning I walked back, past the airport, to Adamas, rucksack weighing twenty-two kilos. No problem. I got the bus up to Pollonia, at the north-east of the island, intending to find a room and make a short day-trip to Kimolos, the adjacent island (I was island-counting at the time), accommodation there being scarce and – naturally – being nervous of being stuck on it. Pollonia was a pleasant place but no one seemed to want to rent out a single room: I tried five places; most only had doubles and the one on offer wasn't ready anyway, for twice the going rate. In a huff, after lunch I got the bus back and the three-thirty 'Express Milos' (ex-Channel ferry 'Vortigern' and showing its age) to Sifnos. (But did see dolphins on the way.)

So it *was* my fault. Had I turned left out of Adamas and gone up the peninsula to the capital, Plaka, the kastro and site of the ancient city nearby might have soothed my irritation. (Oops, back to the question of whether this is for nervous travellers or merely the irritated – and irritating – ones. You've probably already decided.)

So Milos maybe deserves another chance. And Kimolos its first. As for camping, no real regrets. An extra five kilos of weight and clutter to carry versus more comfort for not a great deal more money. But, of course, the end of street cred and the self-image of one in tune with the traditional basic life of Greece (Pathetic, really, ought to stick to Skeggy).

Still, the move upmarket has no doubt benefited the Greek economy (By a few euros?). Too many people try to do it on the cheap. (Guide for the Hypocritical Traveller, too, now? You'd no doubt already decided that)

The next island starts the curve of the circle to the east and is

FOLEGANDROS

Folegandros is one of those smaller islands you warm to. Shaped a bit like a shrimp, it lies east of Milos and, owing to its position between ferry lines, is not easy to reach.

However, in 2007, it was served by one of the Speedrunner catamarans which, according to a plaque inside, was the former 'Hoverspeed GB', winner of the Blue Riband for the fastest crossing of the Atlantic in an earlier life. (Several former British ferries, often cross-Channel boats with previous names like Hengist or 'Vortigern', above, ended up in the Greek islands, partly because, although the EU had a limit of twenty-five years on the operational life of ferries, Greece gained an exemption for up to thirty-five. Don't worry, they're safe enough. Well, mostly.)

Almost as difficult to find at Piraeus as its destination (it was far over to the left beyond the Saronic ferries), Speedrunner was certainly fast, though fairly empty and I doubt it lasted long on the route. It was, however, easy on the nerves.

For many years in the Twentieth century Folegandros was used as an island of exile, with its sheer cliffs, rising to three hundred metres in places, making escape more difficult, and tourism is a comparatively late development. In trying to catch up, there is talk of its becoming an upmarket centre in the Mykonos mould. God help us.

Ferries arrive at Karavostasi on the southeast corner and arrival can be followed by a steep three-kilometre drive up to the main settlement, Hora, perched dramatically on a cliff-top plateau. Consisting of several tree-shaded squares and narrow streets, and with views out as far as Sifnos, Hora is dominated by the hill sloping above it, topped by a whitewashed church a thousand feet above the sea. (It's OK, I didn't venture close enough to peer down. You should have known that by now).

Although it can be breezy in Hora and even cold in the wind in September, its photogenic qualities give the place an immediate attractiveness.

Since the island is barely twelve kilometres long, it is easy to cover it on foot, mainly along the one road that runs along the ridge from Hora to Ano Meria. A diversion to the left a couple of kilometres out of Hora will take you down, steeply, to Angali and the beach, though the way back up is more of a slog. The walk will end at the tiny hamlet of Agios Georgios on the northeast coast and there are footpaths along the way offering short-cuts, or opportunities to get lost. Much of the interior is barren, with abandoned terraces but I did come across an old man ploughing with a donkey.

The ferry ticket office is in Hora, which the nervous traveller will have sussed out, as you'll probably have to walk down to the port and needing to rush back up wouldn't do much for the nerves (though as the ferries are often late, you might survive). My walk down was enlightened by conversation with Jimmy, a young Albanian lad working there, as so many of his compatriots are, in the building trade. Often blamed by Greeks for anything that goes wrong, people who have employed them speak highly of their skills and work-rate.

In the 1880s J Theodore Bent visited the golden grotto, a cave thirty feet above the sea on a 'fearful' path up the sheer cliff below Hora. Not for the nervous ie me.

So, after a relaxing couple of days and a downhill walk, I was ready to wait for the 'Arsinoe' and a short hop to the next island to the east, aligned northeast whereas Folegandros is aligned northwest; slightly bigger but with half the population (a couple of hundred) and an even less-developed feel,

SIKINOS

The wait for the 'Arsinoe' was about three-quarters of an hour, perhaps the small chapel on its upper deck (a not-uncommon feature of older Greek boats but the modern Korean-built ferries have dispensed with them: perhaps they feel less need to pray for deliverance or being on time) holding it back.

There's not a lot to detain you on Sikinos for more than a day (though J Theodore Best was stuck for three in the winter of 1883) but that means it is very peaceful. The ferry port is at Alopronia on the south coast with a newish-looking dock (because it is: thirty years ago you had to land via a small boat) and most of the accommodation is there. It's one of the places where I wasn't annoyed to be accosted for a room and Lucas Rooms, up the hill behind the village, also gave good views.

The only other settlement is the twin village of Hora-Kastro, on the ridge above, along a winding road of a few kilometres seeing little traffic. Both have the traditional Greek village complement of narrow streets and whitewashed houses. Kastro is the larger and brighter of the two, with some impressive mansions around its square. From Kastro steep steps lead up towards the impressive-looking (but closed) walled monastery of Zoodochos Pigi (Spring of Life), set on the edge of the hill with fine views out to sea and dizzying ones down. (Don't…)

Midway between the two villages an old track descends to the road on the outskirts of Alopronia and makes a preferable – and shorter – alternative to the road. Discovering this was useful on the day of departure since, having been too tight-fisted to buy that year's 'Greek Island Hopping', I was under the impression there was a ticket office at the port: as shown in my previous year's copy. Logical enough, new-looking buildings, ideal spot for a ferry ticket office. Too simple.

The ferry was due at 11.30. At 9.30 I wandered down to the shop in Alopronia to ask where the ticket office was. Up in Kastro! Oops. This, however, was where the discovery of the old track came in. From Lucas Rooms I was able to make it up there in thirty-five minutes. Panic over? No chance. I had to ask twice for directions to the ticket office, not exactly hidden away in the warren of alleys but making a fair bid to be. But, having found, it I was back down by 11 and with time to catch my breath before going to wait for the ferry. Nervous traveller saved again.

The ferry was only a quarter of an hour late, which was reassuring as I was aiming for a connexion at Naxos, and seemed to be more or less on time at Ios, the only intermediate stop. However, despite having dropped off most of its passengers there, the last stage was heavy-going and it arrived at Naxos only at 2.45 – the outgoing ferry, the 'Skopelitis', usually left at three. Was I panicking? Of course not.

Two points to note here. Sikinos is where my nervousness went stratospheric. As indicated earlier, an up-to-date guidebook is a help – and even then things might have changed since publication. You can't be too careful. (No, really).

Secondly, Ios. Passed several times and agreeable to look at: the port is attractive and backed by the Hora on the hill behind. But I've never visited. Why not? Its reputation as a wild party island made me too nervous, er, no, that can't be right, can it? I felt it didn't have the right cultural atmosphere to deserve me (Ah, the book's a guide for the Snobbish Traveller now, is it? It's certainly eclectic.)

Homer is said to be buried on the island. This derives from a report of a French explorer a couple of centuries ago saying he'd found a gravestone with 'Homer' written on it. Doubt has since been cast on this claim – though Homer was around – and, as the site is almost inaccessible, it's not been a major tourist draw.

This circular tour of the Cyclades now takes in a few kinks and twists before its completion. Although from Sikinos I was going north to Naxos before heading east to the Small Cyclades and Amorgos, the next stop on this trip turns back to the south of Ios and to one of the most popular – and unusual-cum-intriguing – islands:

SANTORINI

Santorini (or Thira, now the official name) may be spectacular and overflowing with sights and archaeological treasures, but quiet it isn't. The fact that it's still technically an active volcano doesn't put off the hordes of tourists (I couldn't have been paying attention), especially the increasing numbers of cruise ship passengers who flood into the capital, Fira, many of them rushing straight for the jewellery shops.

I first visited Santorini as a starting-off point for a trip to the Small Cyclades, being too nervous to risk Piraeus. It's not actually the quickest way to achieve that aim and wasn't helped by a four-hour delay at Manchester: the plane had a flat battery and it took longer to bring one from Luton or wherever than calling the AA would have done. (Incidentally, if at Manchester you get directed to Gate 300, be suspicious – though it's probably expanded so much by now that it has that many – especially as it turned out to be underground.) So, arrival at Santorini was at 10pm rather than in daylight. A crowd of shouting room sellers almost blocked the exit. I'd intended to camp but at that time of night a change of plan beckoned. (Note the Flexible Trav…)

So, the offer of a room was grasped after some negotiation – she wanted me to pay for the transfer but gave up after I said it was too much. It was in some suburb of Fira lacking any facilities (the suburb, that is, the room was fine) but was, however, close to the bus route to the main port, Athinios, down a winding road a few kilometres south, the first place where it was possible to make a vehicle route down the side of the caldera. (At a later date, on a bus trip from the port to Fira, I was surprised to see what appeared to be *blue* vegetation – be prepared for anything on Santorini. Further inspection showed this, in fact, to be discarded blue supermarket plastic bags snagged in the ground-creeping vines which cover the island.

It is easier on Santorini than at Nissiros to get a sense of the volcano, and its size, since the western coast of the island is the edge of the caldera – the crater – now water-filled. (All that water must have calmed my nerves)

Perched dramatically on this edge, Fira has much to offer, if you can stand/dodge the cruise ship hordes: dizzying views – and ways – down to the old port below, while inland it slopes to the central plain of the island. The bars on the edge of the Caldera are predictably expensive – the insurance probably costs a fortune as, come the next earthquake, they'll be down at sea level – and nevertheless busy. If you want to eat and see the sunset more cheaply – with less worry about earthquakes – there are some tavernas a little way back from the edge that provide these delights.

A path runs to the north along the edge, allowing you the views anyway – of the cruise ships, which have been known to number more than a dozen on some days; of Nea Kameni island in the centre of the bay – a volcanic mass thrown up by later eruptions; and Thirassia, the smaller island that is the far side of the Caldera.

Boat trips round the bay, calling at Nea Kameni and Thirassia, start from the old port below, reached either by the winding steps/donkey track or a cable car. The walk down is pleasant (coming back up is a bit more of a slog) though if you're too tight-fisted (or nervous of falling off) to hire a donkey (5€), your nerves may take another hit when you see a load of donkeys stampeding down towards you – there aren't many alcoves in which to hide. Before you start muttering 'wimp', the word 'donkey' needs an explanation. Forget the type on the beach at Blackpool. Think of a cross between Red Rum and a shire horse. Being mown down isn't the only hazard. If you descend safely, at the bottom you may find the way blocked by a gaggle of these monsters. And no attendants in sight. When this happened, fortunately a girl with experience of horses was at hand and demonstrated the 'four-finger' movement, a kind of neck massage (on the donkey, not you) which allowed you to move them aside without being kicked.

If you've survived this descent (and you'll have to pass the stables at the top – watch where you're walking), the boat trip is well worth it. Even the trek up the lava-covered hill of Nea Kameni to gasp and smell the sulphur isn't that nerve-wracking.

Fira has excellent museums, the Museum of Prehistoric Thira and the Archaeological Museum, again not to be missed. There are also sights at each end of the arms of the Caldera-edge: Oia to the north and Akrotiri to the south.

Oia is an attractive jumble of white-painted houses perched at the northern tip of the island, usually swarming with people and a magnet for those in the evening desperate to watch the sun go down (Very much optional). Akrotiri, while now being developed, is a quieter part of the island and is the location of the amazing archaeological site, only discovered in 1967. Although the new roof gives it less of an atmosphere than previously, it is also unmissable. Make that mind-blowing.

Akrotiri is where I discovered the post-camping preference. I'd camped at Camping Akrotiri, actually on the road towards rather than at, which was sort of closed, ie you could stay but with no evening restaurant. The proprietors were really hoping to develop the site for bungalows. There was a choice of pitch: dusty and soft or drier and firmer. The shower block was modern, with warm showers although some of it had been vandalised. (This is definitely not a guide for mindless vandals. Or any other sort). The nearest taverna was half a mile down the road.

I must have chosen hard and by morning it had added small ants to the attractions. The site breakfast cost more than the camping and I decided to move on. This is where the epiphany came. At Akrotiri, Vagelista's Rooms cost not much more than the camping and came with beds, shower, balcony, fridge and fan. I'd stayed in rooms before, since some islands had no organised campsite but, being dim, hadn't registered the contrast so plainly. (Don't sneer, this is pioneering stuff.)

Besides this, and the site, Akrotiri had a couple of other discoveries. One was Christos, an old Cretan who'd built a delightful, barrel-vaulted house (so earthquake-proof) on the edge of the Caldera twenty-eight years previously, with its own rainwater-collection system. The other, which he introduced me to at Maria's Taverna, was soutsoukakia, for which Maria's was unequalled until Ikaria eighteen years later. Often translated as 'meatballs', soutsoukakia is a sausage-shaped soft rissole-type confection in a tomato sauce. Nerves will evaporate instantly.

Accommodation in Fira is expensive, although on the eastern side of town, down the road to the town campsite, are much cheaper places, while the east coast of Santorini is much quieter, if less attractive. Monolithos has a pleasant, low-key establishment and, although close to the airport, the volume of its traffic is hardly obtrusive. Further south are the resorts of Kamari and Perissia, separated by the hill on which are the remains of ancient Thira. Kamari is, perhaps surprisingly, a tasteful small resort, with views across to Anafi – but no boat trips.

Santorini is also famed for its wines so, while it is hardly a typical Greek island – people racing around on quad-bikes won't ease your nerves – there is more than enough to detain you, and not for a short hop either.

As indicated above, this circular tour of the Cyclades involves some kinks (no, not me; thanks for the insinuation) and that now involves heading north to Naxos before moving eastwards to the so-called Small Cyclades. But, in a further twist (shouldn't this be the Confused Traveller?), before dealing with Naxos, there's a brief visit to its neighbour to the west, and the island ferries coming down from Piraeus touch at first

PAROS

You probably won't remember that my destination on departure from Sifnos was Paros. About half the size of Naxos but still a sizeable island, it's not one I've seen much of, other than a couple of days in the main port, Parikia, still with an old quarter, which was pleasant enough, in order to do a day trip to Antiparos. As a holiday island in its own right, it has attractions and is very popular, though as a hub for further ferry travel, especially to the east, Naxos is usually more convenient.

In antiquity Paros was famed for the translucent quality of its marble and a quarry is still accessible now, though with some difficulty. Boats leave regularly for

ANTIPAROS

About a quarter of the size of its larger neighbour, from which it apparently became detached after an earthquake (don't panic, it was 550BC), Antiparos makes for a pleasant day-trip or a relaxing beach holiday. The boat crossing of about forty minutes lands on the northeast coast at Antiparos Town, the only real settlement, which is little more than a main street with a square and an older part of town, and the remains, though barely visible, of a kastro (look for an arch). A walk across the headland takes about ten minutes, though the main beaches are to the south.

The Antiparos cave, of some repute, is also some way to the south and needs a bus trip. (Caves, bit of a no-no for the nervous)

After this stress-free diversion (if you passed on the cave), it's on to

Naxos

The largest island of the Cyclades, Naxos is immediately striking as you arrive by ferry, thanks to the 3000-foot peak of Mount Zeus (the highest in the group) in its mountainous centre and, as you round the headland into the harbour, the Hora rising behind the port and, nearer, the surviving arch of the Temple of Apollo on the causeway. Also now a popular holiday island, with its own airport (domestic flights only), Naxos has plenty of attractions, both in the Hora itself and across the island. It would be a mistake to see it as merely a hub for onward travel.

Naxos has a number of historical associations and sites. It's the island where Theseus abandoned Ariadne (don't worry, it's not catching. Probably) – his thanks for giving him the thread that enabled him to escape from the Labyrinth in Crete after killing the Minotaur. Fortunately, Dionysus was on hand to look after her (hmm). It was also where Kazantzakis' family decamped to during his childhood when the Turkish pogroms got too vicious, and several places have Cretan connexions.

The Hora, a maze of narrow streets and alleys, is more attractive and interesting than the much-lauded Mykonos. At the top of the hill is the Byzantine kastro, now given over to houses but also with a good archaeological museum. Accommodation is plentiful: the delightful Hotel Anixi is worth the wandering about the Hora to find it – it's usually sign-posted from the opposite direction to yours. On the western edge of the Hora, Rooms Sofi is excellent: the owner usually meets ferries with his minibus. As for eating, Manolis' Garden is worth a visit, although the tavernas along the front are generally good.

Naxos offers plenty of walking opportunities and there is a useful guide with route maps – 'Naxos and the Small Cyclades' by Christian Ucke and Dieter Graf. Apart from the steep ascent of Mount Zeus (no, I didn't either), the going is fairly undemanding, through fertile countryside. A good bus service that runs all the way to Apollonas in the far north enables you to drop off, walk and pick up a return bus later. Filoti is a useful point from which to return as it actually has a signed bus stop (otherwise the nervous traveller will be haunted by the thought that the bus might not stop.) One such walk might include the Temple of Demeter at Ano Sangri before taking you across the Trageia valley – but only if you ask the driver to drop you nearby (I made the mistake of asking the conductor: the message obviously didn't get passed on, so I ended up missing out the temple and starting the walk further along.) The guidebook's timings are fairly generous, so the obvious fear of not making it back in time for the bus is unfounded.

A more varied walk starts higher up at Apeiranthos and is entitled in the book as 'Following in Lord Byron's Footsteps?' (Does the question mark mean he got lost too?) Having found the starting point, I blundered about a bit in the valley (remember one alternative title for this was 'The Dim T…') trying to decide which stream was which before reaching the saddle of the hills, after which all appeared clearer. Lord Byron's connexion is about halfway into the walk, at the abandoned Monastery of Fotodotis, where he is reputed to have scrawled his name in the church. As it was being renovated, with the interior held up by scaffolding, verification was not possible. Apparently, he was so impressed by the beauty of the place he said he wanted to die on Naxos (Be careful what you wish for). From the monastery the route goes downhill and meets the main road (Where, the walking guide says, you can wave down the bus – are they joking?) The alternative, and recommended, as it's an appealing walk, is to take the steps and path leading down into Filoti.

Apeiranthos itself is worth at least a half-day visit. With winding streets, some of them marble-paved, it has a warm atmosphere, even if the temperature – it is a mountain village – is cooler than on the coast. A combined ticket will gain admission to the four private museums, of which the Geological one – Naxos once had extensive emery mines – is surprisingly good.

From Naxos it's on to the Small (or -er) Cyclades, a scattering of mainly diminutive islands to the east and south-east of Naxos. The small car ferry, 'Skopelitis', is the most regular boat serving these islands, making hopping on and off, even on a daily basis, relatively easy. The first island the ferry arrives at, after about an hour and a half, and part of a cluster of four islands separated by very little sea, is

IRAKLIA

The biggest of this cluster (at 17 sq km!), Iraklia is a tranquil place, its main settlement, Agios Georgios, lies on a deep inlet on the north-east coast and straggles up the hill on each side of a ravine.

These small islands are ideal for a two-night stay, giving you a day to do a circular tour on foot. In most cases there's only one route anyway. On Iraklia the route heads south out of Agios Georgios, rising gradually towards Mount Papas, the highest point (and about the height of the Wrekin). Before ascending the mountain, for views of Ios and Santorini, there is a diversion round to the right, to the cave of Agios Ioannis, site of an annual religious festival, which attracts the whole population of the island (100) and which apparently contains an altar. (Naturally I didn't venture inside. Are you surprised?)

From the top of the ridge (stiffish climb) the route crosses to the chapel of Profitas Ilias (as all chapels tend to be known – Prophet Elijah, taken up in fire to God, ie the closest you can get to Him? – though originally Apollo, aka Helios) which actually stands on the edge of a cliff, so you need to circle round to the right to make your way down to the hamlet of Panagia (where, some Germans told me, the taverna has the best-ever saganaki) and then along the road back to Agios Georgios.

There's a sandy beach nearby at Livadi and Agios Georgios has several tavernas with service sometimes as slow as the general pace of life. But, hey, relax.

The next island in the cluster, and barely ten minutes away by ferry, is

SCHINOUSSA

Half the size of Iraklia but with the same size population, Schinoussa's port, Mersini, faces Agios Georgios across the channel, hence the short crossing. From there, the quay consisting only of a clutch of low buildings, (one taverna being the proceeds of the discovery of an antique artefact by the ex-fisherman owner), a tarmac road winds up to the Hora, a one-narrow-street affair, though there is a kilometre-long path that cuts the distance. The 'main' street has a certain charm: if sitting outside the kafenion, you need to breathe in should traffic pass. There's not much of this, although heavy lorries carrying building materials were increasing in frequency even in 2001. (One projected development heralded 'the Valley of the Nine Muses'.)

Schinoussa consists of a series of low hills with tracks leading down between them to small beaches. There's therefore no circular walk, rather a succession of rambles down to the coast then back up to the Hora, along dusty, unpaved roads. On the plus side, everyone you passed there said 'Yas' (hello), even if they were in a car.

The longest walk, to Lioliou beach on the southeast corner, was 2.6 km (signposted). The beach was deserted and the water shallow. On a later visit I crossed from there to the western tip, coming upon closed gates with 'Private' in three languages and pictures of vicious-looking dogs, clearly with no access to the beach. Naturally the sight of the dogs' pictures sent me scuttling away. In 2006 a major police raid uncovered an antiquities-smuggling centre on the island. Can't think where.

Walks to the north lead to the hamlet of Messaria, the odd hill with tower on and the beach of Psili Ammos (also deserted). The main beach below Hora, on the west coast, was the nearest and most developed, so lacking in charm.

However, the most memorable feature of my first visit to Schinoussa was the date: 11th September 2001. The Skopelitis had docked at 7.30am, just as the sun was coming up. The one room seller seemed happy to have bagged a German couple and drove off, leaving me to wander up the path to Hora and sit outside the kafenion with a coffee. The old lady running the kafenion asked if I wanted a room and in due course a woman came to lead us (an Italian couple had arrived) to her upstairs rooms round the corner. While I had been camping, there was no organised site on Schinoussa, so I was open to a room. Mine was narrow, merely a passageway between two iron beds, one of which had a defunct Coca Cola machine at the end. However, the shower did have a curtain and there was a fan so it counted as luxury.

Given the lack of hassle, in the evening I decided to go to the kafenion for a beer before eating. It was quite crowded – two English couples and a pair of old men playing cards. The old lady had to bring out a tin table and chair for me to sit near the door. Glancing inside, there seemed to be some kind of air crash on the TV. My Greek wasn't up to much then, but it appeared to be in the US and involved a skyscraper. The old men carried on playing cards. One of the English couples on the way out asked me about it but I couldn't enlighten them. It looked serious.

Things only became a little clearer later when I went to use the Hora's one card phone. It took some time. A crowd of visitors slowly built up near the phone because it was in use: the island's Romeo was obviously calling his girlfriend – at some length. (For local calls, Greek phonecards, which for an international call gave you three minutes, provided almost unlimited time: it certainly seemed so in this case). Eventually an Italian woman lost patience and shouted at him. His call ended abruptly and he fled.

Mine was also fairly brief: naturally being nervous I'd get the same treatment. Accurate information was limited: in fact, I was told they reckoned there were twenty thousand fatalities (it turned out to be around three). I'm not sure I even knew there were two planes. It seemed shocking enough.

The next morning I went to the kafenion for coffee. The TV news was trying to make sense of the disaster. With little success. However, a group of young Greek workmen sitting in there appeared to find it funny (because it was Americans?). The old lady owner went over and told them off.

Given the amount of development taking place, Schinoussa may be less tranquil than it was; it wouldn't be alone in that. Nerves are not all that's being battered.

From Schinoussa it's a slightly longer voyage to the next inhabited island

KOUFONISSI

Or, strictly speaking, Ano Koufonissi, though it tends to be known in the singular. This is because, sailing from

Schinoussa, the ferry may pass between two more-or-less uninhabited islands, Kato Koufonisi (presumably because it's the more southerly of the two) and the much larger, mountainous one, Keros (almost the size of Iraklia). They're only more-or-less uninhabited because there are a few houses on Kato Koufonissi, mainly of locals who want to get away from it all in summer, but no permanent population, while landing on Keros is now prohibited following the discovery of significant archaeological remains, which are still being excavated.

Koufonissi is the smallest of this cluster, by some way, the flattest and also the most populous. When I was there the coastal path petered out less than halfway round the island (after about 3km) though a circuit may now be possible. Being flat, the walk wasn't exactly gripping anyway. The island's main effect on me, was that it began the fairly rapid decline in my embrace of camping on the Greek islands.

Things didn't get off to the best start. I'd arrived after sunset on the 'Express Apollon', the former cross-channel ferry 'Senlac' (the hill of the Battle of Hastings – not the best omen). Large, old and slow, it seemed to stagger into Koufonissi, where an ancient bus awaited campers. Since bags had to be deposited in a truck there was the added fear for the nervous traveller that he might not see it again. A rocky road ended at a taverna but the campsite was a further hundred yards along the beach. In the dark this appeared to be a vast, desolate expanse of sand. There were, however, some shelters which suggested potential pitches and, with the aid of the head torch, the tent was pitched.

The showers were sea water, hot or very hot, with no apparent way of turning them down or getting them to drain.

The steam also put paid to my head torch (advice to the tight-fisted traveller: buy a decent one).

The taverna wasn't an improvement. It was ten-thirty by then and a piece of thin chicken, very spicy potatoes and open white wine reminiscent of paraffin didn't help the mood. During the night the wind got up and the earplugs I'd been given on Amorgos didn't soften its sound much. There had been plenty of stars though.

Since my ferry departure in a further day's time would involve taking down the tent in the dark (minus head torch), I decided that I needed a room for the next night. That I duly obtained and eventually departed, wondering if these small islands were worth the effort. People on Koufonissi also seemed more stressed than elsewhere.

However, the next island should restore the balance:

DONOUSSA

Out on its own, some way to the north of Koufonissi and opposite the undeveloped east coast of Naxos, Donoussa is only slightly smaller than Iraklia, with about the same population. Like Iraklia it offers the opportunity for a circular walk round the island, of about 16km, that, with a low mountain in the centre, provides more interest than Koufonissi.

The port of Agios Stavros is the main centre of accommodation and there are two other small hamlets around the island. Because of its isolated position ferries are less frequent than at the other Small Cyclades.

However, it was welcoming, exemplified by the family with small children who met with the offer of a room, Ta

Didima (the twins), up the hill above the port. This involved a somewhat circuitous drive in their 4x4, with the little lad driving (on his dad's knee: no, I wasn't nervous either), though the walk directly down to the port to eat only took seven minutes – back up was a bit more of a slog. There were good views from the balcony.

The walking guidebook reckoned the circular walk was about five hours but mine was more like four. The first part of the walk was on monopatia and tracks but apparently the whole has now been tarmacked (providing, in 'Greek Island Hopping', material for a race-track joke at the expense of the island's two cars.) Towards the end of the walk, downhill to Agios Stavros, I seemed to get involved in goat-herding as a woman shouted to me to wave her goats down. They certainly ran away from me though I can't remember if it was in the right direction.

The next island east of Naxos and southeast of the Small Cyclades is hardly 'small':

Amorgos

'Windy' Amorgos, as it's sometimes unkindly called and the most easterly of the Cyclades, is actually a gem with a profusion of charms and challenges. An excellent Topo map, showing marked paths, is an admirable aid to these.

Eight hours from Piraeus by one of the big ferries or five hours out from Naxos on the 'Skopelitis', Amorgos is a smaller version of Karpathos, with a mountainous north, central spine of more mountains and two areas of settlement towards each end of the island. In the case of Amorgos, the road is rather more established and a regular bus service runs between Katapola, the more south-westerly port and Egiali in the north, although ferries often call at both, a legacy of the days in the not-too-distant past before the road link was built.

Egiali saw the start of my camping experience in the Greek islands, chosen because 'Greek Island Hopping' put the site ahead of that in Katapola and the 'Skopelitis' arrived there first. Even so it was 8.30pm on arrival (the boat appeared to be going well with a daylight arrival possible – until it veered north to call at Donoussa, adding an hour in increasingly windy seas) but a 'camping' sign and minibus greeted the ferry so blundering about in the dark only came later, following the instruction 'camp anywhere'. Somehow, I found a space under the awnings which are a necessity because of the hot sun and, with the help of the head torch, managed to erect the tent on the gravel base without destroying those either side.

That done, I found the outdoor showers beneath the stars, with warm water (only the next morning, in daylight, did I realise there were actually showers *inside* the block), the onsite cardphone and the site's attached taverna. Things were looking up…

Until four am, when a sound like machine gun fire woke me with a start. Not good for a nervous traveller in the dark behind a thin layer of canvas. Sometime later there were sounds of people arriving. But no more gunfire. Again, it was the next day when all became clear. The noise was from an arriving ferry in the bay dropping its anchor chain – a common procedure to enable it to swing round on the anchor and slow its approach to the quay. The sound carries too well. Hence also the people arriving.

There was no repeat of the machine gun for the next two nights. But music in the distance and people talking nearby were shades of things to come on Milos. Then there were the donkeys. Loud braying that also sounded as though they were stampeding through the site (but actually a couple of fields away). The problems only reduced after an old couple I met in the taverna gave me some earplugs.

Egiali sits in a wide bay, behind which the mountains rise to their peak at the north of the island and in the folds of whose foothills are two attractive, photogenic villages, Tholaria and Langada. Good paths lead up to both, with one also linking them and making a delightful circular walk of about four to five hours. From both, more paths offer longer or shorter onward routes, though not really anything circular. From Tholaria these walks are shorter – to 'Old Egiali', with wonderful views but few remains, or down a ravine to the bay of Mikri Vlicharda. A longer route goes along the headland and might access beaches (though it was easier to get lost).

From Langada there's short, steep climb up to the windmills on the ridge above the village, with views to islands in the far distance (I thought as far as Ikaria but may be wrong) and a meeting with a donkey train carrying stone slabs on the way down (Shouldn't they have been too tired after that to be braying all night?)

Continuing east from Langada and climbing steadily, you come, after about an hour, to the monastery of Agios Ioannis Theologos (Him again, as at Patmos but I presume this one was just in memory of), which I don't think is open. A right turn here takes you in another forty minutes or so to the little chapel of Stavros, 'on the edge of the precipice', it says on the map. From there you can proceed further, on a narrow path that skirts the cliffs (just remembering it makes me shudder) before climbing onto a level area with the remains of abandoned bauxite mines. (Naturally, with thoughts of the return along the narrow path above vertiginous drops, exploring deserted mine workings wasn't high on the agenda.) However, the views were spectacular and the whole walk full of glorious scents and colours – and a long snake that slithered across the path ahead of me. More than enough for *any* traveller.

At this northern end of the island, where the peak of Mount Horafakia rises to two and a half thousand feet, the land drops precipitately into the sea. In only one place does the map show access, a jetty, presumably the way of shipping the bauxite off the island, but it looks inaccessible now by land.

If these walks seem alluring, there's still the Amorgos signature walk to come – the trek along the spine of the island, from Egiali to Hora (or vice versa, which is probably less demanding in terms of ascent). But, hey, who's a timid traveller here? It's a challenge. (Actually, after the first time, it was more about making the bus).

Naturally, it took me three attempts before I managed it, and that only thanks to some advice from the Germans I'd first come across on Iraklia. Starting from Egiali you begin with a stiff, uphill walk to the other village above the port, Potamos, then continue to climb for the first hour. After that the path levels out with moderate ascents but nothing too steep until the final climb up to Hora.

On my first effort I wasn't really intending to go all the way to Hora, having had a nerve-wracking experience with the bus there the day before (see later) and when I came to a sign saying 'Hora 2"45 (I'd been going about an hour and a half), I decided to turn back. Although a more demanding and dramatic walk, it's less picturesque than the one to the north from Langada.

Attempt two, while staying at Katapola, began with the bus ride (very scenic) to Egiali and the stiff climb. I carried on beyond my previous turning point but somehow lost the path, going too far to the right and following a track that led downhill. In the end, failing to find the correct path, I went down to the road and followed that back to Hora, a longer route. And not only grinding on the nerves.

The following year I finally made it. The advice was to follow the wall and look out for the 'steinmenschen' – stone men, a logical word for cairns really. (Trying to explain where 'cairn' came from failed: I may have claimed it was Scottish). The steinmenschen did indeed save the day; on the one occasion I didn't pick one out at first, I had to climb back up to the path. These steinmenschen weren't measly little piles of stones but five- or six-foot pillars, so deserving of the name anyway (If I've got the German wrong, the Germans explained it was Bavarian dialect).

On this occasion and the following year I continued from Hora back down to Katapola, in all a five-hour trip. (At the start of Luc Besson's film 'The Big Blue', in which Amorgos plays a significant part – so significant that a bar in Katapola plays the video on a continual loop – the kids in the Hora decide to run down to the beach and in the next shot they're there: a good few kilometres, Harry Potter couldn't have done it faster.)

Katapola ('below the town'), the larger of the two ports, consists of three areas at the head of a deep inlet on the north coast of the island. The town it's below nowadays is the delightful Hora, about an hour's walk uphill; the original 'town' it was below is Minoa, an archaeological site, a more taxing but shorter climb. (The name apparently derives from the locals' belief, almost certainly apocryphal, that the Cretan King Minos was buried there).

This part of the island probably has more remarkable sights than around Egiali and as many walking opportunities. The walk up to Minoa, perched on a rocky outcrop eight hundred feet above Katapola, will also enable you to wander round the site: not much has been excavated but the setting is dramatic and the views extensive. There are also a number of paths across the bay (above the area of Katapola known as Xilokeratidhi), some leading down from Hora though, be careful (and this isn't even a nervous traveller-only warning), many of the paths are merely goat tracks that can lead you astray. On one occasion, trying to find a way down, I headed for a chapel on the hillside, reckoning (correctly) that it had to have a track or road to it – modern Greeks obviously wouldn't want to walk. The only slight problem that to reach it I had to cross a ravine (hidden from view until you hit it, as usual), which had a wire fence along my side. Who needs nerves?

Anyway, after this experience I tend to remind myself of the dictum (not mine): 'Always follow the donkey track – donkeys go home, goats just go anywhere.'

The more lengthy routes round here continue past Minoa and there are several possible destinations, though you'll have to return the same way. (There is a bus that serves this end of the island, but it only runs on a Friday)

From Minoa the track descends, passing the deserted and atmospheric, if scruffy, cove of Agii Saranda and then undulates, climbing up and down a couple of hills before ascending to the hamlet of Kamari. According to the map, a path leads off near here to the kastro of ancient Arkesini, one of the three cities of Amorgos in antiquity. Unfortunately, this path is blocked so thoroughly some way along that it even has trees growing through to complete the blockage. To reach Arkesini, therefore, you have to follow the road from Kamari to Vroutsi (only about a kilometre) and then take the path directly down to the site – a gorgeous walk, with a white-painted chapel halfway down and the view of the sea ahead. (It's not quite so scenic coming back up) The kastro is probably more a medieval construction, sited on the older classical base but, balanced on the edge of the cliff (no real fear of falling off, as I recall), it's certainly dramatic.

This is a long return trip, probably a good five hours but you can simply roam up and down the hills for a couple of hours before turning back, if you prefer. From Vroutsi a good path continues towards a fairly well-preserved fourth century BC rectangular 'farmhouse' tower, of which there are half a dozen in the area. Paths and a road continue to the far end of the island though, as a walking trip it's probably too far; however, somewhere along there is the wreck of the ship 'Olympia', which also features heavily in the film 'The Big Blue'.

The next gem on Amorgos is the Hora itself. Set on the crest of the ridge above Katapola, with views to the sea in both directions, its narrow streets running uphill and profusion of flowers give it a warmth and distinction. A shaded square towards the top of the village makes the perfect spot to relax over coffee. Yes, relax – though there is the danger of missing the bus if you're travelling onward. This is aided by the fact that buses don't have any destination signs on the front. Only a problem if there are two buses in the other square at the lower end of Hora at the same time and you're at the back of the queue. Being too timid (in Greek the word for 'nervous' can also have this connotation) to shout out asking which bus I was queuing for, the actual Egiali one, which I wanted, had started off before I got to ask. Cue dash down the road after the driver I'd asked radioed to say there was another passenger. Lesson learned, as they say. (To push in the queue earlier?)

Other wonders await when you walk up to the top of the Hora: first, looking out from the viewpoint to Astypalea ahead and Anafi to the right (these islands always seem fairly close to each other, though it's impossible to cross from one to the other by ferry). Then down a kalderimi to meet the road to Agia Anna beach. What will catch your eye, however, as you look to the left, is the stunning white façade of the Hozoviotissa Monastery. Built into the cliff face that rises up to a thousand feet above the sea, it's one of the most stunning sights in the Greek islands.

You can visit (the Egiali-Hora walk also passes through its grounds) although, of course, the note in 'Greek Island Hopping' that the inside was quite claustrophobic, added to the fear of a rock from high above falling on me (J Theodore Bent suggests my fears weren't as without foundation as you've just decided) has been enough to leave my admiration to the outside. Who says it's what you *don't* do that you regret?

One other experience that Amorgos offered *was* what used to be one of the nervous island-hopper's worst fears: being stuck on an island because the ferries can't run (see Kassos). The modern, purpose-built ferries have to an extent made this a thing of the past, you'll be relieved to know, though some ports still pose problems if the wind is high (see Diafani) and hydrofoils are always susceptible. At Katapola in September 2004 I, and many others, turned up at the quay for the 7am sailing of the 'Skopelitis'. Nothing happened. Nor was any information offered. Eventually it became clear it wasn't leaving – one clue to this is that if the priest gives up, you're stuck. No great problem as I was merely going on to Naxos, but note the advice in 'Greek Island Hopping' to avoid leaving your departure from a remote island to the day you're due to fly home. (Oh, my God, something else to worry about). Later that afternoon wind was blamed.

The same thing happened the next day. This time the word 'Bofor' was muttered. (the Beaufort scale of wind strength is much used in Greece. When Fanis, the proprietor of the 'The Big Blue', came down, this was clarified as Bofor 9 in the Central Aegean (seven caused a diversion from Diafani on Karpathos once) so no ferries were running. It might go at 7pm or, more probably, the next day.

The next day, at 7am, still no joy. Or news until 8.30 when midday was a possibility. That became five. Ironically, on 'windy' Amorgos, all was fairly calm, but it was the ferry's onward route causing the delay. Even more ironically the wind strengthened during the afternoon so at 4pm the boat began to load. (My notes say it was the former Cross-Channel ferry 'Hengist' but its Greek name is lost, as will *it* be by now).

There is a book from the time of the Junta by an ex-politician, exiled to the island by the Colonels, entitled 'Escape from Amorgos'. But, frankly, who'd want to?

If Amorgos seems out in the middle of nowhere, one of the islands visible from the viewpoint at the top of Hora really is.

ASTYPALEA

A butterfly-shaped island to the southeast of Amorgos, Astypalea **is** miles from anywhere. If you sailed directly south from it and just missed the east coast of Crete the next landfall would be Egypt. Technically a member of the Dodecanese islands, Astypalea has more in common with and is more easily accessed from the Cyclades. Its Dodecanese membership derives from the fact that, on Greek independence in 1830, the maps were so poor it ended up on the Turkish side of the divide.

Seeing it out there in the blue from Amorgos had given it an allure, but I then took about twelve years to pluck up the courage to risk a visit. Getting there had never seemed easy. There is a twice-weekly ferry from Kalimnos, from where Astypalea is administered, to the older, and central, port of Pera Yialos but the big ferries from Piraeus (increasing in number), via Amorgos, use the new port at Agios Andreas, seven kilometres from the older one at Pera Yialos (and with no facilities or ticket office – Nervous T, note). Given that these ferries tend to arrive in the middle of the night, the chances of being stuck there appeared considerable (though, in practice, minimal. Even if there wasn't a taxi free, it wouldn't take long for one (of the island's two) to come back, but who's to know that? Don't blame my nerves.)

The answer was to fly (Yes, OK, but don't forget about the islanders' livelihoods).

Had I looked closely into that, I might have opted for the 3am possible abandonment instead. (Astypalea has the endearing characteristic of feeding your worst nervous fears while also offering complete peace and quiet). Aegean check-in at Athens airport can resemble the first day of a sale at a major London store and finding that the plane is a 19-seater propeller job may not calm the palpitations (don't worry, it flies at only fifteen thousand feet so, apart from the good views, you'll have less far to fall).

Sitting in the back seat might also not have been the best move for the nerves, especially on landing. Descending almost to sea level, the shoreline appeared remarkably close, and somewhat high, as the plane just about lifted onto the land.

From then on everything calmed. On these small island airports, it's a short walk to the terminal and your luggage may even make it before you. A waiting car from the hotel (it was the middle of the day) soon had us at the harbour-front Paradissos Hotel in Pera Yialos.

Most of the population lives on this, western, wing of the 'butterfly'. Pera Yialos, a fairly modern place, is small, with a handy beach and some excellent tavernas. It then extends up the hill to the attractive Hora, reached by stepped paths and dominated by the ruined kastro, even more distinctive when it's lit up at night.

The kastro aside, if Astypalea can seem smaller-scale and less dramatic than Amorgos, that's because it is, but its warm charm quickly infuses you and you might forget you were ever a nervous traveller (you'll remember soon enough).

It's possible to walk round the western 'wing' in about four hours, mainly on roads though some are 'dirt' in places.

The only car that passed me stopped and I was asked if I needed anything. At the western end of the circuit the path climbs over the ridge before descending towards Livadia, the other main resort with views of the far side of the kastro from Pera Yialos.

Leaving by ferry will bring a return of the tremors. You'll be worrying (a) whether the alarm will go off at 3.30am and, more particularly (b) if the taxi will turn up – of course, he will, it's his livelihood.

But even in your half-awake stupor, the sight of a brightly-lit Blue Star monster, engines throbbing, in the dark emptiness of Agios Andreas port will settle your concerns.

It's about two hours to Egiali, with dawn coming up over Kalymnos at about six and then the majestic, towering cliffs of the northern tip of Amorgos watching you pass.

Moving on from way out in the depths of the Aegean and the Cyclades, the next group of islands begins not far south of Athens and a brief mention of the capital's delights needs to come first. While clearly not an island, it may not only be your gateway to many of them, but also is worth a stay in its own right and requires a few words, and recommendations, here.

ATHENS

Clearly, being caught up in the bustle of a mega city is likely to bring on the heeby-jeebies (normal people call it excitement), especially when everyone warns you of pickpockets. Tip: stay alert (as if you wouldn't) and watch out in particular for little, eastern-European-looking women (not that I'm prejudiced and that was in Italy anyway). The metro from the airport is said to be a fertile hunting ground. (The service, though, is excellent, if crowded; just remember, if travelling *to* the airport from Athens that you need an airport ticket (about 10€): looking at the price tables, it's easy to think you only need one for a single stop. (Is it, or is this the Dim Traveller re-emerging? Safest thing is to buy from a kiosk, if there is one.)

Things not to miss:

1. The Acropolis opens at 8am. Be there. You won't be alone, but the crowds will be slightly less; if you want to be first, get there at 7.30. Or 7. Or 6. Being there early means you'll see the soldiers coming to raise the Greek flag. Don't forget to wander down behind

the Erechtheion to view the descendant of the Sacred Olive Tree.

2. The new Acropolis Museum. Our excuse for not returning the Elgin Marbles was always that Athens had nowhere decent to show them. Now they have, we're saying we bought them anyway. If we had any decency (no chance, then), we'd swap them for copies since the originals filling the gaps would restore the impressive frieze to its former glory (smile at the rather sarky comments where there are gaps, saying 'in the British Museum'). Don't miss the outdoor section of the café, with views of the Parthenon. Another bonus of an early start. (But warning for the nervous: the sloping glazed walkway up from the ground floor of the museum covers archaeological remains uncovered during building: you may feel queasy glancing down).

3. The National Archaeological Museum. Stupendous. Not in the most salubrious part of Athens and probably best reached by a fifteen-minute walk from Omonia metro station (a taxi would be simpler but you'll have heard about their reputation for overcharging). Emerging from the station it can be difficult to get orientated. I asked a group of policemen: most hadn't a clue. On reflection, I decided they were probably MAT (riot police. Years earlier I'd been cursing the Athens air pollution, until I came across a MAT riot bus – it turned out there'd been a demo and this was the remains of tear gas. Don't panic, no need to take a mask; not a gas one anyway).

The profusion, and quality, of the exhibits is breath-taking and, if you start to flag, there's an excellent café in the basement (despite the pigeons that fly in and out). The most mind-blowing exhibit was the Antikythera Mechanism, a kind of four-thousand year-old computer, found in a shipwreck off the island from which it takes its name.

4. The Agora. You can wander around, taking in the Theseion, a temple in a good state of repair, and the cells where Socrates drank the hemlock (don't panic, they're not enclosed, you can't get locked in or be forced to drink hemlock. On second thoughts, if they hear you griping, some people might be tempted to try the last).

From Athens either a metro trip or the airport bus will take you to Piraeus for

THE ARGO-SARONIC ISLANDS

The first of these, reached either by hydrofoil in about forty-five minutes or, preferably, in a couple of hours by traditional ferry, which allows you to savour the vastness – and merchant shipping – of the Saronic Gulf (you'll also pass by the island of Salamina, behind which in 480BC was fought the Battle of Salamis, one of the most significant sea battles in history), is:

AEGINA

Almost a suburb of Athens, its main town and port, Aegina Town is a bright, lively place which retains its charm. Just to the north of the town is the interesting archaeological site of Kolona, a former Temple of Apollo, identified by its one surviving column, and next to it an excellent museum.

The town is very much a working environment, with many small shops and businesses in the back streets, besides catering for visitors. It has a range of restaurants, from the basic to the more sophisticated and the front is lined with bars and cafes, allowing relaxation with views of the sea.

Towards the other side of the island, after a pleasant half-hour bus ride that passes a huge monastery complex, very popular with Greek passengers, is the small Temple of Aphaia. Thirty years ago you could walk around inside, although now it is fenced off and, while fairly complete, if you've recently visited the Parthenon, it can seem underwhelming. The adjacent museum is often closed.

The island is renowned for pistaccio-growing and much of it is verdant. A more tranquil base from which to explore Athens, should your nerves be frayed there.

A few minutes to the west by hydrofoil or ferry is Aegina's smaller neighbour,

Angistri

If Aegina is too populous and lively for you, Angistri, a small, pine-covered island, should provide adequate calm. It makes for a relaxing day- or half-day trip, on the way to Aegina, especially if your hotel check-in is later in the afternoon. A couple of large island map boards at the ports display a walking route across the island, so activity opportunities shouldn't be lacking were you to stay longer.

Arrival at Skala, the main ferry port on the northeast coast, is a restrained affair. The relaxed atmosphere is almost palpable, the only (mild) excitement provided by the arrival and departure of the ferry.

Then follows the obligatory anxiety, as you discover that hydrofoils, for return to Aegina, don't leave from Skala but from Mylos, around the coast. That must be all of a couple of kilometres away. A bus timetable indicates that there's a bus shortly. But where's the bus station? Panic now. (Wilfred

Owen's 'an ecstasy of fumbling' in his poem 'Gas Attack' had nothing on this.)

There is, of course, a town map and a short walk round the corner will reveal the diminutive bus. As with most panic situations, they turn into opportunities. In this case, to see another (small) part of the island by bus and then to sit under a tamarisk tree by the beach looking out over the Peloponnese mountains opposite.

If you weren't already on your way somewhere else, it would be easy to succumb to the gentle charms of Angistri and prolong your stay. Nerves, forget them.

The next island, a little further south and almost attached to the mainland, is

POROS

An island only touched on, usually on a three-island tour out of Athens, the regular ferry links to Poros (and Aegina) don't seem to feature on ferry websites – perhaps because the locals know where to find the info anyway, so where's the need?

Nor did there seem to be any service calling in at Aegina on its way to Poros. More difficult to visit than Astypalea? Hmm.

Its waterfront looked attractive on a brief promenade and there's an extensive archaeological site inland.

So, only on the must-do-it-properly-one-day list.

That leads on, round the foot of the 'thumb' of the Peloponnese, the southern Argolid, to

HYDRA

A narrow, rocky and largely uninhabited island, Hydra

became fashionable in the 70s (Leonard Cohen, among others, lived there) and today is a much-visited (from every direction) trendy and pricey destination, though the Lulu Taverna, uphill from the front, proved both good and inexpensive for lunch.

Hydra owes its popularity and attractiveness to the dramatic location of Hydra Town, the only settlement, rising behind a horseshoe-shaped harbour crammed with yachts, tour boats and ferries. Half the time, it's so busy, tour boats have to drop their passengers and then cruise about at sea to make space for new arrivals.

Walking around the back streets or round the harbour are the main activities on a day-trip ie a couple of hours. A longer stay may exhaust your goodwill and walking in the interior doesn't sound too exciting – even a non-nervous walker may not enjoy a lack of paths and shade. But Hydra's worth seeing. (Oh, and there is no hydra – many-headed snake – so hang loose, only the jewellery shops might devour you.)

A day-trip from the Peloponese will probably also call, further southwest, at

SPETSES

Smaller and less dramatic than Hydra, Spetses is also a one-town island, with cars banned (as on Hydra) though mopeds make up the noise. Its role in the 1821 War of Independence is its main claim to fame, with a museum dedicated to the revolutionary heroine Bouboulina and memorials to the Declaration of Independence. So, a stroll along the front past the Old Harbour and back up and round to the centre is pleasant enough. The only stress-danger is worrying if your tour boat will leave without you (apart from the fear of being knocked down by a scooter in a pedestrianised street).

Most of the island is wooded and became popular in the 80s with literary-minded Brits since John Fowles' 'The Magus' is set there.

A longer stay would probably involve beaches or walks through the woods, although the mainland town of Kosta is close and served by frequent ferries, so organised trips to classical sites on the Peloponnese are available.

Prior to the cutting of the Corinth Canal, the Peloponnese was not an island but in view of that it can now qualify, without even resorting to the excuse used of Pelion. Though that excuse would be more than justified, if the Corinth Canal didn't mean there was now water on all four sides.

PELOPONNESE

In fact, the ending of its Greek name, 'nissos' acknowledges that to all intents, the Peloponnese was an island before it was completely severed. Its vast area, covering an area almost a quarter of mainland Greece, could easily absorb you for several weeks or visits and for every kind of activity.

It's also relatively easy to get to, since the airport at Kalamata is served from several UK provincial hubs, while some good (and sparsely-trafficked) motorways mean that travelling around is fairly stress-free.

History abounds on the Peloponnese, from the dawn of civilisation to more recent upheavals. If you stay at Nauplio (two hours northeast of Kalamata) or its nearby seaside resort of Tolon (Sunvil's Stella Apartments on the beach in the latter are highly recommended), visits to Mycenae, Tiryns, Epidaurus and Argos are easily possible by bus.

Nauplio is a delightful town, with a broad central square surrounded by imposing buildings. Briefly the capital of independent Greece (1827-34), its first Prime Minister, Capodistrias, was assassinated here in 1831 (it's said the bullet hole in the church door he was standing beside can still be seen). Dominated by the Palamidi Castle on a two-hundred metre-high hill (the claimed 999 steps up is probably an exaggeration but feel free to check) and surrounded on three sides by sea, the narrow streets of its older quarter make for relaxed wanderings. There are several interesting museums, an almost four-thousand-year-old suit of armour in the archaeological museum probably the most stunning exhibit.

Mycenae (Mykines in Greek) sits on a rocky hill above the plain, with higher mountains behind, and needs to be approached slowly to appreciate the drama of its position – a tour bus might take it at too much of a rush and dump you high up in the car park, from where you may wonder what that little bump is all about: because it is a relatively small site – and many people will come, infused with its role in the Trojan War and subsequent events much featured in Greek tragedy, expecting some vast metropolis. Reality can often fail to live up to the power of myth. (It's also best visited in a morning, before crowds of Greek schoolkids descend upon it). Seen from the right perspective, it is a remarkable sight.

As is, if to a lesser extent, Tiryns ('of the great walls': Homer?). Beside the road to Argos, about three miles north of Nauplio, Tiryns doesn't have the same dramatic setting as Mycenae but the walls are undoubtedly impressive.

It would be easy to neglect the archaeological site at Argos, close to the town centre, where the theatre, rising steeply up the hill, can look more imposing than that at Epidauros. An excellent archaeological museum in the pretty central square was closed in 2017 for an unspecified time. If re-opened, it shouldn't be missed.

The theatre at Epidaurus is much-visited by documentary-makers eager to demonstrate its amazing acoustics, though as at Mycenae you need to approach from the right angle ie frontally, to get its full grandeur – the path from the car parks comes on it from the side.

If staying in Tolon, a short walk along the coast will bring you to the archaeological site of Asine, again with links to the Trojan War, which has recently been much improved and displays a George Seferis poem (in Greek) about its king.

Going north from Kalamata through the mountains, a delightful hill village in which to stay is Andritsena, where the Hotel Theoxenia provides bright hospitality, and the tavernas simple but delicious village fare. Nearby, well, 14km into the middle of nowhere, is the Temple of Bassae (not visited, had a puncture), said to be one of the best in Greece but under a concrete cover and even so deteriorating. There's also a famous library near the hotel (closed as it was a Monday).

From Andritsena the road leads north to Olympia, a site redolent with history and pleasant enough to wander round but lacking any of the dramatic grandeur of the Parthenon or Delphi (even I couldn't swing it to classify that as an island – visit nonetheless). The museum, however, should not be missed, especially for the sensational metopes, an indication of what the Elgin marbles could look if returned in situ. There's also a two-and-a-half-thousand-year-old helmet to take away any breath you have left. Staying in the nearby village of Pisses at the small Hotel Bacchus should soothe any remaining nerves from the drive up to Olympia, though the 8km of unmade road beyond Andritsena may have been tarmacked by now.

Following the coast road south from Olympia, you reach, after about three hours, the delightful coastal town of Pylos. Situated in a bowl of the hills on the almost enclosed

Navarino Bay, site of a decisive battle of the Greek war of Independence in 1827, when a British-led fleet destroyed the Turkish naval force, it has a large tree-filled square and, from the sea-front Hotel Miramare, wonderful views across the bay.

A boat trip round the bay calls at the memorials to the various allied national contingents from the battle: the French and Russian being on the island of Sfaktiria, which encloses the bay, the British on a small island in the centre. There's a good museum of the battle near the harbour in Pylos.

Sfaktiria itself was the scene of another famous battle, in 425BC, between Athenian and Spartan forces during the Peloponnesian War. Nearby is the so-called Palace of Nestor, another major player in the Trojan War.

Heading east over the mountains from Kalamata for a couple of hours will bring you to the dramatic site of Mystras, the last capital of Byzantium after the fall of Constantinople. Mystras, which is being 'restored' with Evans-like zeal, overlooks the valley of modern Sparta, though of the ancient city virtually nothing remains.

(A more modern history of the area, during the Civil War of 1946-9, can be found in 'The Flight of Icarus' by Kevin Andrews, an American student with a grant to study castles of the Mani, who found himself drawn into hearing about the internecine struggles, which were particularly vicious in the Peloponnese. The resulting work – the castles got forgotten – is one of the best travel books on Greece.)

The Taygetos mountains, rising up to eight thousand feet, dominate this part of the Peloponnese and, heading south from Kalamata, the village of Kardamyli gives access into them via the huge Viros Gorge (walking up this many years ago, two large dogs came charging round a bend ahead. I nipped quickly up a bank as they shot past. Nervous traveller status quickly confirmed).

Kardamyli, thanks to its associations with Patrick Leigh Fermor, who lived there for many years, has become rather twee recently but it also stands on the route down to the south, the Inner Mani, a barren area long cut-off from the rest of Greece and regarded as a land of evil, 'kakovounia' – the bad mountains. (Calm down.)

On the outer edge of this, you come to the town of Areopoli, 'city of the war god', so re-named after it became the place where the Greek flag was first raised to start the revolution against the Turks in 1821. The house where this occurred can be seen down the street from the pleasant main square, which is dominated by a huge statue of Petrobey Mavromichalis, one of the leaders of the uprising.

One of the features of the Inner Mani is the proliferation of tower houses, built for both defence and attack – the higher your tower, the more easily you could pour fire down on your neighbours. (In one of his more shocking anecdotes, Kevin Andrews describes how neighbourliness in this region hadn't improved over the centuries.)

Years ago, in a small village museum in the Inner Mani there were two framed photographs of men lying on a road, clearly dead. When I asked the curator what these photos were, he shrugged and said scornfully, 'Huh, Bulgarians.' (Don't worry, but keep your passport handy.)

Clearly, all this violence won't have endeared the Mani to the nervous traveller, even if it was all in the past. Better leave the Peloponnese and head smartly south to an actual island more likely to soothe the fevered mind:

KYTHIRA

At first sight, from the air, scrub-covered Kythera doesn't look that impressive.

However, on closer acquaintance, its rolling hills and deep ravines, together with an absence of heavy touristic development, give it a restful charm.

Reputedly the birthplace of Aphrodite, Kythira is situated not far south of the easternmost leg of the Peloponnese. It has not been that readily accessible from the UK, since the more frequent ferries ran from Neapoli on the southern tip of the Peloponnese and the less frequent between Kissamos in western Crete and Piraeus. Not only that, the new port of Diakofti lies in the middle of nowhere (shades of Astipalea) on the island's east coast. The nervous traveller's nightmare.

However, a complicated package with Sunvil, via Athens, with a short flight and pre-booked taxi, overcame these limitations. Next time, Diakofti is to be risked, from Crete. Who says nervous travelling is incurable?

One endearing aspect of Kythira is that the people actually like the British and speak highly of the period in the mid-nineteenth century when we administered the island –

a legacy of the Napoleonic wars, Napoleon having destroyed the Venetian Republic, under whose auspices Kythira (and the Ionian islands further north) had lived for centuries. Even before Napoleon's fall, we picked up the islands as part of the fallout from the disintegration of the Republic and, in a departure from the usual colonial mindset, not only seemed to go down well with the islanders – establishing an education system and building bridges still in use today – but actually gave the island *freely* back to the Greek state in the 1860s. Taxi drivers proudly point out the 'English bridge' as you cross it. Would they do that in Skegness?

A further, intriguing, British link to Kythira, then known as Cerigo, occurred during World War One in 1916. At that time Greece was neutral, being wooed both by Germany, whom the King favoured, and the Allies, whom the Prime Minister, the Cretan, Venizelos, favoured; the two coming close to civil war over the issue. Kythira, a supporter of Venizelos, was effectively being crushed and starved by the royalist Peloponese, on whom it depended. A British naval intelligence officer based at Souda in Crete (there in neutral territory merely to facilitate cable traffic through the Mediterranean, you understand) arranged for a boat to drop pro-Venizelist gendarmes on Kythira to grab control from royalist elements and ensure its survival.

Another, more recent indication of the mutual warmth, was the unveiling on the quay at Kapsali in 2015 of a memorial to the crew of the cruiser, HMS Gloucester, sunk south of Kythira, with huge loss of life during the Battle of Crete in 1941.

Kapsali, on the south coast, is the major tourist resort and, except in August, is a sedate place (again with its British relic, an aqueduct, though only the tank at the bottom survives, looking much like a large bunker) The Hotel Porto Delfino, on the hill above Kapsali, provides warm hospitality and fine views out to sea and the rocky outcrop of Avgo – with a further connexion to Kevin Andrews: he drowned in 1989 while swimming out to it, possibly having had an epileptic fit, to which he was prone. The cliffs behind the hotel feature a tiny monastery high up on the side.

Hora, the most photogenic site on Kythira, mainly thanks to its Venetian Kastro, overlooks Kapsali and can be reached by a winding road or – preferably coming down – by a footpath that's quite steep in places. Both routes cross a shorter 'English' bridge than the longer one further north.

Hora is a quiet, friendly place, with small, picturesque square and a superbly laid-out and modern archaeological museum that gives a comprehensive view of the island's history. The kastro itself is more impressive externally: within there are a couple of chapels but not much else that's open, although the views are glorious.

At the eastern edge of the island, the small seaside village of Avlemonas sits on a narrow inlet and has an excellent fish taverna. The drive there from Hora allows the attractiveness of Kythira to unfold as the road winds through the rolling hills and pretty villages (and across the major English bridge!). Descending to the coastal plain before Avlemonas, in the distance can be seen the mountain on which a Minoan peak sanctuary has been found. A stiff walk up to the nearby chapel of Agios Georgios sto Vouno gives fine views of the coast. (The heat may deter the nervous.)

An interesting 'British' connexion to Avlemonas is that the ship carrying the Elgin Marbles was wrecked off the nearby coast. Kythiran divers recovered the treasure: with hindsight, perhaps not the most helpfully patriotic of moves.

A further excursion from Hora is to the north and the pretty village of Mylopotamos, with walks to old watermills. The Anavasi Terrain map shows a number of other walking trails but getting to the start point, as on Ikaria, requires either a car or taxi.

As Kythira grows on you, so will the urge to return, nerves forgotten.

A dozen or so kilometres to the south of Kythira lies Antikythira, a small, rocky island with a permanent population of under fifty and reached by infrequent ferries. Its claim to fame is the Antikythira Mechanism, found in a shipwreck off the island and now in the National Archaeological Museum in Athens. As indicated above, mind-blowing.

These two islands stand, very much apart from any others, between the Peloponnese and Crete. The chain, as part of which they were traditionally administered, lies far to the north, off the western coast of Mainland Greece:

THE IONIAN
ISLANDS

Given that the Ionian islands are strung out from near the Albanian border to the northwest corner of the Peloponnese, it's perhaps not surprising that Kythira was administered with them, as its distance south from the southernmost, Zante (omitted here, as its party reputation has never attracted), is not much further than Zante's from the northernmost, which is:

CORFU

Tapering off to its south and so shaped rather like a tadpole, Corfu (known as Kerkyra in Greek) was also one of the earliest Greek islands to be developed for mass tourism and so some areas, especially on the east coast, have been blighted by unsightly hotel building. However, it is a very green island and there are regions, especially the northwest, where tourism remains fairly low-key, at least by comparison.

Corfu Town is an excellent place to stay, elegant, with a number of sites of interest and pleasant walks along the promenade on the wide bay. Again, there's evidence of the British influence, not least in the town centre cricket pitch.

The Old Fortress, jutting out on a promontory into the sea, generally loses out to the New Fortress in terms of architectural interest but has a good deal to reward the attention: a Byzantine Museum near the entrance, a scattering of barracks and an acropolis with extensive views. The Old Palace was also alluring, if rather overwhelmed by Japanese influence. In 2016 the Archaeological Museum was closed for refurbishment. (As was the home of the poet Solomos – open am only)

Continuing round the headland to the south of the town, you come to 'Mon Repos', birthplace of Prince Philip and now an interesting museum, besides having attractive gardens which include a Doric temple and ancient trees.

The Old Town has many imposing buildings, often of faded elegance, and a variety of eating establishments, ranging from the seriously upmarket to the simpler, traditional Greek outlets. If your nerves need shopping therapy there's also an M&S.

There is a Corfu walking trail, running most of the length of the island, but it doesn't seem to have taken off. When it was launched, the guide to it wasn't published in time, which may not have helped.

In the far northwest corner of Corfu, the small resort of Arillas has a hospitable feel and good beaches. Just up the coast from it, via an interesting cliffside path, is the slightly larger and rather faded resort of Agios Stephanos (West, apparently, there must be a few of them). From here day-trips are possible to three small satellite islands. The nearest and smallest of which is:

MATHRAKI

Mathraki, where you get an hour and a half to explore, is about forty minutes west of Corfu. A short walk uphill brings you to Kato Mathraki (the map provided by the tour company showed Ano Mathraki to be further on) but as the tavernas there evinced no sign of life, it was a return to the port taverna for coffee. The map also showed a surfeit of 'old ports' (three) on the north coast, possibly one for each household. It could hardly be described as a stressful place. Loggerhead turtles nest on the island in the summer, so presumably they know a peaceful spot when they see it. One caveat for the nervous nostrils: the weed clogging part of the harbour did have a pungent smell and there seemed to be plenty of mossies around. Then on to:

OTHONI

A further fifteen or so kilometres north west, Othoni is the largest and the only one that has a resident tourist population in the summer. (Don't panic, you won't be swamped: it probably means five Swedes at peak time). The map showed a number of inland villages but as the interior seemed hilly beyond the port, Ammos, it didn't look feasible in the two and a half hours' stay, not least because the proprietor of the pleasant beachside taverna ('Nostimon Imar'?) insisted on cooking his fresh moussaka, which was actually delicious and the wait proved very restful.

It's said that, if you're contemplating a longer stay on one of these islands, you should decide and book on the evidence of such a day trip.

The third, Erikoussa, wasn't included on this trip, and boats seem to go mainly from Sidari, the bigger and more boisterous resort on the north coast of Corfu.

So, getting-away-from-it-all is not difficult here and there are probably many more options. It is also possible to make a trip to Albania from Corfu Town, though clearly you'll be too mindful of its criminal associations to risk it.

An historical footnote regarding Albania: following the First Balkan War in 1912-13 the Great Powers set on creating a new state of Albania. The question was where to draw its southern boundary with the part of Greece, Epirus, also newly-liberated from the disintegrating Ottoman Empire. The ethnic Greek area stretched to the north of Corfu and the Greeks had no wish to be joined to the Albanians, whom they regarded as uncivilised (a prejudice that endures today). However, at the Versailles Peace Conference of 1919, Italy demanded that the border be moved further south to avoid Greece's having control of the Narrow Corfu Strait. So, a mass of ethnic Greeks ended up in Albania and, eventually, in the ultra-Marxist regime of Enver Hoxa.

South of Corfu, though also reached via the mainland, are two small islands:

Paxi/Paxos

That's one island, the names are interchangeable. Barely twelve kilometres long but with masses of olive groves and towering cliffs on the west coast, Paxi attracts upmarket British tourists and loads of day-trippers, the latter usually not making it beyond the main port, Gaios Town. Paxi does, however, make a pleasant destination for a day-trip – from

Parga on the mainland or the longer trip down from Corfu Town, with obligatory visits to beaches, particularly on the even smaller, satellite island of Antipaxos to the south.

Probably, therefore, an ideal spot for the nervous traveller who likes a bit of walking, though, as it's the most expensive, there may be pain in the wallet instead.

The next island south – and a considerable way south – is also a day-trip opportunity and joined to the mainland by a bridge:

LEFKADA/ LEFKAS

(The islands round here seem to favour alternative names, a leftover from Venetian influence.) Most boat trips (from Kefalonia in this case) put in to the port of Nidri for lunch (the captain's recommendation will no doubt turn out to be his cousin's place), having stopped at Meganissi, just off the southwest coast, for coffee and then lingered off Skorpios, the Onassis private island, to gaze at an empty tree-backed beach. It was rumoured that armed guards were once employed to deter invaders but as the line has died out there was no sign and a few hardy souls (excluding guess who?) swam to stand on the beach and feel… rich? Cursed? Lucky?

Onassis managed the last of these in Smyrna in 1922 when, although eighteen, he persuaded the Turks he was younger and so was allowed to leave, avoiding the massacre in the destruction of the city. Cursed, in that his son was killed and his daughter decamped, leaving him only with the consolation of his wealth, though having abandoned his great love, Maria Callas, for Jackie Kennedy maybe even that had a bitter taste. So don't bemoan your nerves; be careful what you envy.

MEGANISSI

Dropped at Spilia on the north coast it was either a quick trek up the cliff to Spartohori (ten minutes, though it's not clear if that's up or down) or coffee by the beach: coffee won. A destination for Sunvil packages, the island gave a positive first impression and would be attractive for a longer visit were life not too short.

From Lefkada it's not much further south to two adjoining islands, the larger, first, being

KEFALONIA

The largest of the Ionian islands, Kefalonia tends to be regarded as a more sedate version of Corfu. In part this is because its tourist development came later, avoiding some of the worst excesses of the rush to open up. Whether this was because of the islanders' insularity or the after-effects of a severe earthquake in 1956 is an open question.

Dominated by the five thousand-plus peak of Mount Enos in the south, Kefalonia has plenty of greenery and many attractive beaches. Tourism tends to have spread between different areas, allowing most to retain their own way of life (minus much traditional architecture, destroyed in the earthquake). In recent years the book and film of 'Captain Corelli's Mandolin', the latter shot on the island, have brought many people to look for the locations. (The beach south of Sami, where the Italian prostitutes danced, is worth visiting in its own right). In Greece the book caused much controversy over its depiction of the Left in WW2.

Fiskado in the north is one of the most attractive towns on the island, partly due to its relative survival of the earthquake. From here, across the strait, lies the small, mountainous island, rich in myth:

ITHACA

The supposed home of Odysseus, Ithaca is an easy day-trip destination from Kefalonia but anyone coming to see archaeological relics of the hero is likely to be disappointed. One or two locations are claimed to fit descriptions in Homer but actual evidence – even of a palace – has proved elusive, leading some to suggest that larger Kefalonia could be his actual home (though when you consider the relatively small size of many mythically important sites – Mycenae, for instance – Ithaca's role may be more believable; and we are talking of the mythical past, remember)

A day-trip is unlikely to permit more than stops at a couple of ports – Frikes or Kioni – and the capital and main port, Vathy, set in a deep and narrow inlet which gives it a dramatic location, if no grand home of Odysseus. (Someone I knew was brought to Ithaca every year for his family holiday when he was young. He claimed that after a week he'd had enough as there was only so much swimming you could do. Nerves didn't seem to have been his problem.)

So, another island to soothe the ruffled soul (if you avoid the clifftop drive to Stavros) and the poem 'Ithaca' by C.P. Cavafy could provide a fitting epitaph for the nervous traveller's wanderings:

'… don't hurry the journey at all.
Better if it lasts for years
So you're old by the time you reach the island
Wealthy with all you've learned on the way,
Not expecting Ithaca to make you rich.'

But the nerves having been soothed away by the experience.

WHERE NEXT?

Evia – Covid permitting (at the third – or fourth? – attempt)
Kythnos – missed through irregular ferry connexions.
Lemnos – Gallipoli link but a Gatwick job and package?
Anafi – too difficult to get to and not be stuck on?
Skyros – via Evia but a long trek for Rupert Brooke's grave.
Samothrace – another long trek
Hios – doesn't grab me somehow.
Agathonisi – long way to go for a short stay.
Ios – do I really want to see Homer's grave?
Agios Efstratios – that would be just for boasting.

Besides: there are the ones to *re-visit!* Crete, Karpathos, Amorgos, to name a few. To keep (nerves-free) travelling because

> 'every hour is saved
> From that eternal silence, something more,
> A bringer of new things…
> To sail beyond the sunset and the baths
> Of all the western stars…'

Beyond the what? That was OK for Tennyson.

As a nervous traveller, who are you kidding?

BIBLIOGRAPHY

Kevin Andrews	The Flight of Icarus
J Theodore Bent	The Cyclades or Life Among the Insular Greeks (1885)*
John Bishop	Love, Freedom or Death
Michael Carroll	Gates of the Wind/An Island in Greece…
CP Cavafy	Poems
Dominique Eudes	The Kapetanios
Nicholas Gage	A Place for Us; Eleni.
Giorgos Harokopos	The Abduction of General Kreipe
Colin Janes	The Eagles of Crete
Roger Jinkinson	Tales from a Greek Island (& More Tales…) American Icarus (A biography of Kevin Andrews)

---

* Now available from Forgotten Books

Nikos Kazantzakis	Zorba the Greek; Report to Greco; Freedom and Death
GC Kiriakopoulos	Ten Days to Destiny
Elias Kulukundis	The Feasts of Memory
Mark Mazower	Inside Hitler's Greece
Frewin Poffley	Greek Island Hopping 2013 (and earlier)
Giorgos Psychoundakis	The Cretan Runner
Anthony Rogers	Churchill's Folly
Rough Guides	To Crete/The Greek Islands
Mikis Theodorakis	Journals of Resistance
Peter Trudgell	In Sfakia
Christian Ucke & Dieter Graf	Naxos and the Small Cyclades
Loraine Wilson	Crete: the White Mountains

All errors in this book are mine alone.